The Complete Communicator

"IF MY POSSESSIONS WERE ALL TAKEN
FROM ME EXCEPT ONE,
I WOULD CHOOSE TO KEEP
THE POWER OF COMMUNICATION—
FOR BY IT I WOULD SOON
REGAIN ALL OF THE REST."

—*Daniel Webster*

The Complete Communicator

Change Your Communication—
Change Your Life!

William Lampton, Ph.D.

HILLSBORO PRESS
Franklin, Tennessee

Printed in the United States of America

03   02   01   00   99   1   2   3   4   5

Library of Congress Catalog Card Number: 98-75588

ISBN: 1-57736-133-4

Cover design by Gary Bozeman

Published by
HILLSBORO PRESS
an imprint of
PROVIDENCE HOUSE PUBLISHERS
238 Seaboard Lane • Franklin, Tennessee 37067
800-321-5692

TO

THE THREE Ss

SANDRA
SHELLEY
SUZANNE

My wife and daughters, whose
communication with me enriches my
life beyond a writer's ability to describe

CONTENTS

PREFACE

ONE OF MY MOST MEMORABLE LESSONS IN THE ART of communication happened in the first grade. My twin brother Ben and I told our mother which classmates we wanted to invite to our birthday party. She agreed, and instructed us to ask these friends individually during the next week.

However, I chose a way to spread the word more quickly. Telling Mrs. Griffith I wanted to make an announcement, I stood and said, "Ben and I invite the following people to our birthday party." Then I read the list aloud. When Mrs. Griffith called Mother, they expanded the party plans to include the entire class. Without delay, Mother taught me that the quickest way may not be the best way.

Have you endured similar repercussions from your communication efforts? I imagine so, because communication blunders occur in spite of our good intentions. Maybe, as I illustrated, we don't predict audience reaction accurately. Maybe we forget the impact certain words will have on people. Or we use the right words, but contradict them with our facial expressions and tone of voice. Yes, we mean well—but we make harmful choices.

I have written *The Complete Communicator* to address the communication challenges we confront in a variety of situations. You'll notice an absence of academic references, though you might expect footnotes and a bibliography from a former university faculty member. In their place, you'll find easy-to-understand, easy-to-apply references taken from my kaleidoscopic career—including teaching at the University of Georgia and the Atlanta Federal Penitentiary, radio and television broadcasting, acting, writing for newspapers and magazines, speaking, consulting, and directing workshops.

Years ago, I wondered why speakers and writers talked and wrote so much about their own experiences. Now I have the answer—that's how and where we learn the most! Academic credentials may form the framework, but *vital education* takes place where we live and work and play . . . among real people facing complex interpersonal and organizational communication opportunities.

The subtitle *Change Your Communication—Change Your Life!* states my motto. I can verify this promise from what has happened for me personally. Of equal significance, I have seen lifestyle improvements among those who have joined me in learning more about communication, at conferences, conventions, and workshops.

In essence, all our relationships depend upon our communication skills. By reading *The Complete Communicator*, I hope your relationships—with yourself and others—will improve daily.

As a coach, I want to know the players. Feel free to get in touch, to share *your* communication experiences and insights with me. Like my model teacher Socrates, I roam the marketplace asking plenty of questions. I'll welcome your answers.

ACKNOWLEDGMENTS

WRITERS SPEND AN ENORMOUS AMOUNT OF TIME working alone—reading, outlining, writing, rewriting, mailing to editors, making revisions, and at last sending a completed work to the publisher. Yet despite their prolonged solitude, most authors acknowledge that others have contributed to their success. I'm among those who recall, with immeasurable gratitude, people who taught, inspired, and encouraged me—believing I had a message and the ability to share my thoughts on paper.

Sandra, my wife, first read my writing in the form of love letters to her as a teenager. Apparently, the letters were effective. Throughout my career, she has served as a valuable ally—evaluating article ideas, proofreading, and editing. In the midst of her responsibilities as a second-grade teacher, she assisted me every evening during the writing of this book, critiquing the drafts and recommending improvements. Truly, the book became a duet, rather than a solo. With heartfelt appreciation, the dedication page gives tribute to her and our daughters, Shelley Jenkins and Suzanne Derrick.

My mother-in-law, Ora Watson, has provided light and laughter for many years, along with words of encouragement.

Prior to his death, my father-in-law, Horace Watson, limited himself to few words—but invariably they were words of kindness and compliments.

Before establishing my own household, I began my lifelong affection for great literature, following the example of my parents, George and Nelle Lampton of Columbia, Mississippi. They served as cheerleaders for my writing and speaking. Though I cannot present them with a copy of this book, I thank them for their love—and for lessons which endure long after our physical time together ended.

My brother Ben and sisters Jane Conerly and Anne Walker continue the support our parents initiated.

Dr. Paul H. Boase, my dissertation director at Ohio University, helped channel my passion for writing. No graduate student has had a finer mentor. Beyond our professional association, he blesses me with his friendship.

Joel Williams—station manager in charge of programming at South 106.1 Radio in Gainesville, Georgia—helped me develop and market my radio program, *The Communication Corner*, through his coaching, technical expertise, and influence. He's a premier announcer I am proud to know and work with.

Other family members, friends, teachers, and professional colleagues have expressed faith in my future, and have offered much-needed advice. Although I can't name every person in my network, you know who you are.

Thanks to editors and publishers who have included my articles in newspapers and magazines. Your acceptances encouraged me to continue writing.

I extend genuine appreciation to Andy Miller, Mary Bray Wheeler, and the entire staff at Providence House Publishers and Hillsboro Press. I feel so privileged to join the list of authors who are fortunate enough to work with you.

Special gratitude goes to my readers. You compliment me by selecting my writings from among so many possibilities. As we establish a friendship on paper, I hope we'll have opportunities to know each other personally as well.

1

PERSON TO PERSON

CALL SOMEBODY A "TERRIFIC COMMUNICATOR" AND your listeners are likely to picture a person holding a microphone, addressing a large audience with enviable eloquence. However, that's an exaggerated picture, for we spend most of our communication time in *person-to-person* presentations. Examples:

Rapport-building chitchat with a customer who's in our place of business for the first time

Conversations with employees in the lunchroom

The annual company holiday dinner, where we want to make the right impression

Our volunteer organization's monthly board meeting

Sales calls on prospects and current clients

Settling family discord

Discussion of major news items with associates

This opening chapter identifies and explains the basic elements for successful person-to-person communication. They're worth reading about. They work.

TALKING TO YOURSELF

MOST PEOPLE THAT I KNOW WANT TO EXCEL IN *interpersonal* relationships. They'd love to walk into a room filled with strangers, and not feel extreme anxiety about conversations. They fantasize about greeting customers and creating a climate of goodwill. On the larger public scale, they dream of speaking to an audience jammed with eager listeners. More personally, they envision family encounters that are open, genuine, mutually supportive.

During my university faculty days, I offered a noncredit evening course called "Improving Your Conversation." Nearly thirty people enrolled—salespeople, housewives, and a television broadcaster were among them. During the sixteen hours we met, participants wanted to find new attitudes and habits which would lead to more fulfilling interaction with others.

We concentrated on what we should change about *ourselves.* By the second week, we agreed that in order to jet propel our *interpersonal* communication, we must begin with our *intrapersonal* communication. No mystery here . . . just recognition that *self-talk* paves the way for talking with others.

At the end of the course, one woman told me: "These eight weeks helped me gain a new concept of who I am. When I came in here, I had just gone through a divorce. My self-esteem was low. I doubted my ability to reenter the social scene. I felt shy, afraid. However, learning to reach out to *myself* has changed everything. That makes it possible for me to relate to others."

Dr. Shad Helmstetter, my favorite contemporary author on this topic, titles his book *What to Say When You Talk to Yourself.*

Early in the book, he says children hear the word "no" more than 148,000 times—"considerably more negative programming than any of us needs." What's the long-range damage? By the time we're adults, we have become accustomed to accepting a defeatist attitude. To what extent? Helmstetter reports, "as much as 77 percent of everything we think is negative, counterproductive, and works against us."

Likening the human brain to a computer, he advocates getting rid of our harmful mental programs, and bringing in healthy, affirmative ones. Repeatedly, he urges us to "erase and replace."

Envision two ways of handling the same scene.

First response: You've made the short list for a job you want desperately. One hour before the big interview, you're reviewing the job description and forecasting the questions you'll hear. Suddenly, dubious self-talk begins:

"What am I doing here? I'm not qualified."

"I know the other finalist—much more attractive than me, a really smooth talker."

"I'll be satisfied if I don't embarrass myself too much."

"Bet they won't like this old suit. Should have bought a new one."

"That interview with the rival company bombed. Wonder if this interviewer heard about that fiasco."

Unmistakably, you're setting yourself up for failure, with *self-fulfilling prophecy.*

Second response: These are your thoughts:

"Man, glad I got the degree I did. Makes me a perfect fit for this position."

"Interviews don't scare me. Yeah, some haven't been winners, but everybody has a few bad ones. I've gotten this far professionally because I'm poised and articulate during interviews."

"Ted is a capable finalist. He'll present himself well. Yet worrying about him accomplishes nothing. I'll forget the competition—and concentrate on the opportunity."

"What if I didn't buy a new suit? This one represents contemporary style. The personnel officials will like the physical impression I make."

That, too, is *self-fulfilling prophecy.*

To echo Ralph Waldo Emerson: "Trust thyself: every heart vibrates to that iron string."

Whenever a scheduled conversation, meeting, or speech brings up self-defeating thoughts, change your self-talk. Talk to yourself as you would to a best friend or a child—as a coach, encourager, fan, believer. Your interpersonal communication will blossom beautifully.

SUPPRESSING THOSE STEREOTYPES

BOTH AT WORK AND IN OUR PERSONAL LIVES, we'll improve communication by suppressing the influence of stereotypes. As you know, a stereotype occurs when we make a judgment about a group, without recognizing individual exceptions to the group's general reputation.

Note these examples: "All teenagers are irresponsible." "All college coaches are breaking NCAA recruiting rules." "All bosses are just out for themselves." "All wealthy people are selfish."

Look at the key word which begins each sentence—the word "all." Another stereotype tipoff is the word "every," such as "Every single person is lonely and maladjusted."

Have you ever felt you were a victim of stereotyping? As women have moved into managerial posts, they have referred to a "glass ceiling"—the result of the stereotype which questions their ability to assume corporate leadership at the highest levels.

I'm an identical twin. Throughout my childhood, I had to fight the stereotype that my brother and I thought exactly alike, and wanted to do exactly what the other did. Those assumptions were way off base. For both of us, going to separate colleges established the personal identity other siblings

4

enjoyed all along. Even today, although we share a few interests and ideas, our differences outweigh our similarities.

Understanding how severely stereotypes distort reality, I propose two ways of improving interpersonal and organizational communication.

Number one: Constantly reexamine our tendency to categorize people. Let's check ourselves when we start to say "all" and "every." Look around for exceptions. You'll find them, once you open yourself to acknowledge their possibility. Reword your sweeping general comments.

The change calls for eliminating harmful phrases. Discipline yourself to stop saying, "Why, that's just like a . . . ," referring unfavorably to a race, nationality, gender, religious body, or profession.

Number two: Assert ourselves in challenging categories others put us into. Suggest politely, "You're mistaken in your opinion about me. Let me tell you why." Years ago I heard the observation, "all labels are libels." There's wisdom in those words. With tact and goodwill, you and I can resist accepting the labels we don't fit. We'll win respect, and will enjoy fresh opportunities for unblemished communication.

THROUGH YOUR LOOKING GLASS

THE EDITOR SUGGESTED BY PHONE, "LET'S MEET for lunch. We'll discuss your writing project then."

"How will I know you?" I asked.

"Oh," she answered, "that's easy. I'll be the tall, skinny blonde."

I formed a mental picture—but one destined to be short-lived. For on that Tuesday, when she walked up to greet me, I was glad she spoke first. I wouldn't have identified her from the description. In fact, I'd glanced at her once, then looked elsewhere.

She seemed average height, with light brown hair, and not all that skinny (which, of course, I couldn't mention).

Everybody has similar experiences. Written and spoken descriptions seem even less reliable than weather forecasts and lottery tickets.

We hear, "Great movie—you have to see it!" We rent the video, then cut it off after ten minutes, muttering, *"This movie got an Oscar?"*

You dislike the "super restaurant" a friend raved about. To you, prices were too high, servers were slow and rude, and you'd rate the food bland, at best.

As a result, we have popularized statements like "Beauty is in the eye of the beholder" and "One man's meat is another man's poison."

Communication specialists attribute these diverse interpretations to *perception*. They explain that each of us has a unique *window to the world*. Consequently, our viewpoints are truly customized, like a contact lens prescription which works for us, but not for the person standing next to us.

Life experiences shape perception. A Boston native will laugh at the Atlanta weatherman's "frigid" forecast that temperatures will dip into the 40s. Bostonians wash their cars on those days.

A person's needs alter perception. You've heard the advice, "Don't go grocery shopping when you're hungry." You'll buy foods you'd bypass when shopping just after a meal. Also, think of driving past a bank sign and seeing the time and temperature flashing alternately. Running late for an appointment, you're likely to focus on the time. Heading for the beach, you'll center on the temperature. In either case, the irrelevant numbers might not "register" with you. If asked, you couldn't repeat them.

Gender influences perception. Often we feel there's no exaggeration in John Gray's title, *Men Are from Mars, Women Are from Venus*. As Gray states, many male/female conflicts don't revolve around issues of right or wrong, but around opposite vantage points.

Certainly economic status alters perception. What, for instance, is your definition of an expensive house? Think back to when your salary was one third or one half of your current income. Your dollar figure for an expensive home was radically different then, wasn't it? Throw in how housing prices have escalated in the last twenty years, and you'll note another reason definitions change.

Physical characteristics play important roles. In the sixth grade, I learned that I'm largely color-blind. Maybe the editor I met for lunch really was more of a blonde than I thought. Also, were I shorter in stature, she could have fit the "tall" description.

You could add to the list of factors which affect perception—age, various roles we play, tradition, family values, national and ethnic origin, education, religious beliefs, and more.

There's an important lesson here—both for communication and human relations. In his autobiography, Benjamin Franklin spoke to this point. Late in life, he adopted a new way of dealing with people. Abandoning the dogmatic style of his youth, he started using these phrases: "the way I look at this," "it seems to me," and "I could be mistaken, but . . ." Franklin noticed radical improvement in his communication efforts and how he related to others.

Examine your looking glass—the porthole through which you see the world and its inhabitants. Realize how and why your individual window is unlikely to match another person's. Expect the differences in what each of you sees, and then says. Allow for discrepancies—and learn from them.

An old saying confirms Franklin's advice about perception: "Don't call the world dirty because you forgot to clean your glasses."

BEWARE OF ASSUMPTIONS

JUST FOUR MONTHS AFTER GRADUATE SCHOOL, I was surprised my dissertation director, Dr. Paul Boase of Ohio University, was calling me. We exchanged greetings, then reached the purpose of the call.

"I have a nice surprise for you. I've learned that the fellow-ship you held included payment for typing of your dissertation. We can arrange reimbursement if you'll send receipts."

"Send them? I'd hand deliver them if necessary. I *like* this surprise! How long will the process take?"

"Shouldn't be long. The financial aid office is set to process your request. I predict a quick turnaround."

Two weeks later, the words "quick turnaround" seemed to repeat themselves mockingly, especially during the trips I made to my faculty mailbox with increasing frequency.

At the end of the third week, my tolerance for waiting expired. If you've ever awaited a sizable check in the mail, you empathize with my feelings. A time or two, I dreamed the envelope had made its way to the box.

I picked up the phone, dialed, asked for Dr. Boase. "He's not here now. Want to leave a message?"

"Yes, I do," I answered, making sure I maintained an even tone. "Please let him know I called to ask about the status of my refund check."

"Sure," she promised.

Heading for lunch, I felt relieved. Just hearing the familiar voice of his secretary helped. He'd understand my concern. With his characteristic courtesy, he'd reply, probably today.

An hour later, I bent to peer into box number eleven. Good, a phone message, on a pink slip covered by Elise's unmistak-able handwriting. I pulled out the message page, and read:

Tell Dr. Lampton I Didn't Know He Is So Greedy

I read the note a second time. The words had not changed. I did, though. My face reddened, a tightness gripped my throat. Lowering my head, I walked around the corner to my office. Shutting and locking the door, I glared at the note again. These thoughts came to me, almost audibly:

"I thought I handled the matter tactfully. Where did I go wrong?"

"Our relationship was so special. He was more than a professor and mentor. He was a friend and supporter. Now I've lost all that."

"What now? Will I still get the money?"

"Will he accept my apology? But for what?"

"It's doubly embarrassing because Elise took his message. Maybe she has spread word around our department."

The more I thought, the bleaker the scene became. I dreaded carrying this bad news home. But I couldn't go home yet. Two afternoon classes to direct. Students must have seen my distraction. Afterwards, I made the office my sanctuary for brooding.

Suddenly, a revelation came. I was not interpreting the phone call, I was reacting to *a report of the phone call*—indirect evidence. Funny, as a faculty member in communication I urged students to go beyond *content* to evaluate *intent*. I had failed to do that.

Marching to Elise's office at twice my normal pace, I was glad to find her alone.

"Elise, I have your note about the call from Dr. Boase. *This one*," handing the page to her.

"Yes, I remember the call, earlier today."

"Well, Elise, I need your help. I'm not trying to put you on the spot, believe me. But this is important. How did he *sound* when he mentioned me being greedy?"

"Sound?"

"Right, sound. Was he upset, did you catch a sign of hostility?"

Her pause increased my suspense. When she laughed, I detected no sarcasm. She kept laughing as she answered, "Oh, just the opposite. He was laughing hard. Must have a real good sense of humor."

"So he was just kidding me?"

"Absolutely! Sorry you weren't around to take his call. You'd have laughed, too, I'm sure."

As I thanked her and turned to leave, she added: "He said they mailed your check today."

Incredible! Because of a misguided *assumption,* I had let my imagination run amuck. The negative thinking which resulted made me question the most important professional relationship I had experienced. Equally as damaging, I pictured the end of a friendship. In almost paranoid fashion, I forecasted the loss of money which was rightfully mine.

My considerable anguish taught me an unforgettable lesson: *Beware of assumptions!*

Check them out. Draw inferences from facts, not supposition. Verify presumptions before deciding and acting.

True, we can rely on some assumptions—those we base on oft-repeated interactions.

When you have *any doubt at all*, though, search for verification.

Dr. Boase, I'm glad you chuckled when you called me greedy.

THE VALUE OF FEEDBACK

LET'S THINK ABOUT A SIMPLE COMMUNICATION exercise I present in my workshops, with the help of two volunteers.

The first volunteer tries to get the workshop participants to draw a geometrical design. This presenter works under tight restrictions—not allowed to face the audience, use gestures, or answer questions.

How does the presenter know when to quit? Sheer guesswork. Without visual contact, there's no way of knowing whether listeners look lost or content. Without questions, the speaker has no sense of "I got it" versus "I'm lost."

The second volunteer communicates without these restrictions. She faces the audience, maintaining steady eye contact. She answers questions. Although she cannot use a visual aid (a restriction in common with the first speaker), gestures help convey shape and size. As a result, this presentation prompts greater participation than the first. We call this audience response "feedback."

The first setting involves *unilateral,* or one-way communication. The second demonstrates *bilateral,* or two-way communication.

Which method consumes less time? Unilateral, because only one person has permission to talk. Ordinarily, unilateral averages no more than half the time of bilateral. Because I have taught numerous workshops on time management, I'm all for conserving time. Even so, with what we gain in time, consider what we lose.

Accuracy suffers greatly without feedback. The bilateral group will score three to four times higher than the unilateral group. In fact, the unilateral group experiences plenty of amusement when the exercise ends, and participants compare their efforts to draw the design. Sometimes no two listeners come up with similar sketches . . . and almost none resemble the original.

The unilateral group undergoes far more frustration than the bilateral group. Members exhibit their frustrations in several ways. Despite the ban on discussion, a few members will ask for clarification. The presenter has to restate the rules. Then new signs of frustration surface—moaning, mumbling, and physical unrest—shifting, slouching, rolling the eyes upward, and even putting the head on the desk, as if to say "I quit."

Questionnaires administered to both groups point to higher morale among bilaterals. They know someone is listening, they are confident of the information they receive, and they appreciate the speaker's interest in getting the message across.

The bilateral/unilateral exercise causes us to reconsider habitual comments about meetings.

"Quick meeting, didn't waste time." Possibly—but did participants value brevity above accuracy and contentment?

"Quiet, orderly meeting. Very few said anything." Granted—yet maybe the format discouraged participation.

"Everybody seemed to agree." Oh, really? I think "seemed" becomes the definitive word.

How much one-way communication exists in *your* organization? In meetings, interviews, performance appraisals, and other settings, do leaders encourage and welcome feedback?

When you *maximize* bilateral communication, you'll *maximize* teamwork, morale, and efficiency.

Don't you consider these advantages worth the extra time?

WHAT'S YOUR STYLE?

DR. DEBORAH TANNEN, A NOTED LINGUISTICS professor and popular author, says in the preface to *That's Not What I Meant* that we learn to use language as we grow up. Because we grow up "in different parts of the country, having different ethnic, religious, or class backgrounds, even just being male or female—all result in different ways of talking, which I call conversational style."

Illustrations of style variations surround us.

Harry Golden, a newspaper publisher, moved to Charlotte, North Carolina, from a northern state. I enjoyed reading his account of his first weeks in the South. Right away, adapting to the language style challenged him.

He wrote about meeting people, having a friendly conversation, and hearing them say, "Why don't you visit us sometime?" Interpreting them literally, Golden opened his calendar and replied, "Well, looks like next Tuesday night is available. What time do you want me to arrive?"

After a few incidents of this sort, he became aware he had spoken inappropriately. From the shifty glances, nervous coughs, and litany of excuses he saw and heard, he gained fresh perspective. Understanding that cultural styles foster unique rituals for communicating, he deciphered the invitations this way: "We like you, and we hope there will be other opportunities to get to know you."

For another example, how do you feel when you greet somebody with, "Hi, how're you doing today?" and they give you (in expanded detail) the latest report from their doctor and stockbroker? They describe an argument with a neighbor. They complain about the weather.

They mistranslated your question. In your mind, your question meant, "I'm glad to see you. Let's find a pleasant topic that interests both of us."

Americans who travel abroad have happier trips when they get tips about prevailing language rituals. When my wife and I made our first trip to a country where shoppers bargain with merchants, a hotel concierge cautioned us to avoid paying the first price mentioned—*even if we liked the price and were ready to buy the item.* To skip the bartering phase would offend the seller, although the bartered price would of course drop from the original. Once we adopted the new language ritual, we had fun extending the transaction far beyond our custom.

Again, the person who spends her life in an open culture, where people ask each other about personal matters, runs the risk of being called "nosy" in another setting. That's not her intent, only what her unfamiliar conversation partners perceive.

What's your language style? What rituals became your habits, even in childhood? The more clearly you answer those questions, the more readily you'll reduce misunderstandings with others . . . as, simultaneously, you discern their communication styles.

THE FINE ART OF SAYING "NO"

IN THE BROADWAY MUSICAL *OKLAHOMA*, A CHARACTER named Ado Annie sang, "I'm just a girl who can't say no, I'm in a terrible fix."

She's right. This incredibly short word—*no*—can accomplish so much. Inability to use the word causes a multitude of problems.

Bosses who can't say no are headed for trouble. Sure, if you grant every request, you'll make everybody happy . . . but only temporarily. Why? Because everyone can't take vacation time the same day (such as a long weekend leading up to a Monday holiday). Somebody has to stick around to keep the doors open.

When I left university teaching and became manager of a department, my first few months bordered on absolute chaos. I wanted to play Mr. Nice Guy, agreeing to whatever any employee requested. Initially, workers loved me. Then they saw how my "yeses" contradicted each other. Until I learned to say "no," my credibility hit bottom.

The employee who says nothing but "yes" loses out. You'll take on too much to handle. Also, your supervisor may spot you as an individual with no self-identity. Although you're perfectly agreeable, management will pass you over at promotion time—for just that reason.

In the family, if you say "yes" halfheartedly to a beach vacation—though you prefer the mountains—your disappointment will surface, now or later at the beach.

Lack of honesty threatens friendships. "Want to play bridge?" a neighbor asks. If you agree, yet despise playing card games, problems will occur.

You may ask, "How do you say 'no' without damaging relationships?"

Let the person know you respect his or her statement or request, and that your decline isn't personal.

Explain why your refusal benefits both of you. For instance, when you decline membership on a committee, tell the chairman, "I can't accept because I'm going to be traveling extensively for the next several weeks. If I accepted, I couldn't attend or do any volunteer work. My decline helps you more than my acceptance would."

Invite the other person to participate in the decision. Stephen Covey, in his splendid book about management and communication, *The Seven Habits of Highly Effective People*, tells about his experience as director of University Relations at a large institution. He asked one of his creative writers to take charge of a new project. The reply was, "Stephen, I'll do whatever you want me to do. Just let me share with you my situation." The writer asked Covey to view the writer's wallboard, which listed projects, along with their deadlines and performance criteria.

"Stephen," the employee said, "to do the jobs that you want done right would take several days. Which of these projects would you like me to delay or cancel to satisfy your request?"

"So," Covey reports, "I went and found another crisis manager and gave the job to him."

Saying "no" with courtesy and tact won't offend others. And you'll avoid that "terrible fix" endured by Ado Annie.

TELLING IT LIKE IT ISN'T

DO YOU REMEMBER WHEN YOU HEARD "TELL IT like it is" for the first time? Although sportscaster Howard Cosell didn't originate the phrase, he used it often enough on *Monday Night Football* to create widespread usage. Americans declared they would start speaking frankly and bluntly, without apology.

But that doesn't happen often. Most of the time, we tone down the impact of harsh circumstances—by using mannerly, soothing words that won't offend listeners. We call these words "euphemisms."

Business and professional people have coined numerous substitute words to avoid saying "You're fired." They classify the released worker as downsized, dehired, outplaced, or re-engineered, supposedly because "the position no longer fits our organizational structure." Sounds kinder, right? Unfortunately, there's still no paycheck next week.

The Wall Street Journal reported that some unfortunate workers misunderstood these camouflaged messages. In some cases, they came to work the next day, thinking their supervisors had given them only a warning.

At all levels, educators soft-pedal reality. Students no longer fail, they are "underachievers." Classrooms aren't bothered by brats, just "socially maladjusted children." The most expensive colleges aren't overpriced, they "require careful financial planning."

Again, does anybody admit "I'm broke"? No, they're "experiencing cash flow problems," "operating on deficit financing," or "temporarily insolvent."

Notice that the tougher a situation becomes, the more gently we speak. "She died" becomes "she passed away." Rather than being "dead," she's "late." So beware of the dentist who warns, "This may sting a little"; the mechanic who suggests, "Your car engine needs some attention"; and the appliance repairman who admits, "My estimate might be slightly conservative."

Euphemisms allow us to say what should be said, without alienating listeners. After all, it's easier to use substitute words than to repair shattered feelings.

INFORMAL COMMUNICATION BRINGS BIG DIVIDENDS

W E'RE FAMILIAR WITH THE FORMAL OCCASIONS for recognizing and thanking employees. Companies establish programs for employee of the month and employee of the year, with generous benefits for honorees, ranging from parking privileges to banquets to cruises. Through these structured programs, employers communicate "You're important," "Your good work makes a difference," and "We appreciate you."

I applaud these efforts. When employees perceive the awards criteria as fair, recognition becomes a strong incentive for improved performance. Recognition boosts morale.

Too, I applaud *year-round, informal recognition*. Weekly, even daily recognition, costs little and requires no authorized plan. Managers just do it. Because informal recognition is spontaneous, receivers may feel there's more sincerity demonstrated.

One example would be inviting an employee to lunch. The company cafeteria provides an acceptable place, although hosting the employee in a special atmosphere seems more like a treat.

You don't need an agenda. In fact, you don't want to "talk shop" very much. Now's the time to ask about the employee's family, hobbies, vacation plans, and personal goals. These topics indicate your interest in the worker *as a person*. Remember the old way of referring to workers as *hired hands*? Impromptu lunches on a casual basis help prevent this impression.

Also, become highly visible in the organization. Employees enjoy seeing supervisors "out and around." Conversations with the boss aren't as threatening when the employee stands on *home turf*. I remember one CEO who shielded himself from employees by using a private passage into the building. The silent message spoke rather loudly about his attitude. More positively, all of us have welcomed managers who "drop by."

Another suggestion: Send handwritten cards and letters for special personal occasions—graduations, engagements, weddings, anniversaries, births, deaths, athletic achievements, civic leadership, and publications. An employee will remember your thoughtfulness for many years.

I emphasize *handwritten*. Computer-literate people are suspicious of a typed letter—possibly "canned," with the same letter reused, changing only the name of the recipient. Handwritten appreciation suggests "this one's for me only."

A popular song from the 1950s claimed, "Little things mean a lot." They still do in communicating with employees.

COMPLIMENTS ENRICH RELATIONSHIPS

I'M CONVINCED THAT PRAISING OTHERS WILL ENRICH our communication, and our relationships as well.

Consider your workplace. When was the last time your boss praised you, or you congratulated a colleague? Can't remember either one? Then it's time to start spreading words of appreciation.

Try these constructive examples: "You seem to be more comfortable conducting meetings these days." "I like the way you served that customer." "Good job on those letters you drafted. You've got the feel of my writing style now."

Years ago, a manager told me, "You have to be careful, Bill. I've learned not to compliment my people. Makes them too self-assured, and they get lax in their work habits." Fortunately, managers of his ilk comprise a minority. Savvy supervisors have learned the value of a proverbial pat on the back.

The home scene needs tributes, too. For instance: "That dessert was really delicious." "You look extra sharp today." "I'm proud of you for doing your homework without my reminders."

In social settings, your hostess will welcome, "Coming up the driveway, I noticed the new landscaping. Really improves the entrance to your property."

Well, how do we keep our compliments from becoming flattery? The guidelines are easy:

Offer compliments which reflect your genuine feelings. We have a tendency to answer a compliment with, "Oh, you can't mean that!" (hoping they really do). Possibly we've run across an abundance of compliments which smacked of artificiality. Listeners detect shallow praise. When you *have deep convictions about your positive appraisals, people will sense your authenticity.*

Give realistic compliments. If somebody told me, "Bill, you're quite a dancer," I'd laugh out loud. Sadly, so would my wife.

Issue compliments in moderation. Just as Lady Macbeth "doth protest too much," individuals can lose credibility by praising excessively. Refrain from becoming fulsome—and family, friends, and co-workers will know they earned your admiration.

Use compliments in proper context. We suspect the employee who follows "You're such a fair boss" with "By the way, I want the afternoon off."

When you gain a reputation for offering genuine, realistic compliments in moderation, and in the right framework, you'll notice your associates responding positively. In fact, they'll compliment *you* for your thoughtful expressions.

COMMUNICATING THROUGH COURTESY

THE PIGTAILED LITTLE GIRL ON THE COMMUTER train saw the man drop part of his newspaper as he walked by. Instantly, she bounced to her feet, picked up the section, caught up with him, and—without a word—handed the paper to him.

The man thanked her graciously. She went back to her seat, grinned, and put her head in her mother's lap. The mother patted her daughter, and smiled approvingly.

Watching the child's thoughtfulness in action brightened my day. I enjoyed seeing proof that people still communicate through courtesy. My inclination was to thank the mother for passing courtesy along to the next generation.

At times we wonder whether somebody held a funeral for good manners, and we didn't get an invitation. When the store clerk says, "You need to make up your mind. I have other customers waiting," when drivers won't let us turn across traffic despite our blinking signal, when the cashier says he's "too busy to make change for a phone call," or another couple barges into the restaurant line—we grow skeptical. We ask, "Has communicating through courtesy disappeared?"

Thankfully, hopeful signs appear. I've noticed the growing number of consultants who teach etiquette classes. Professional people enroll because they want guidance for their conduct at lunches, dinners, dances, and receptions with executives—and sometimes with their spouses. In the words of Terry Wildemann, a consultant based in Rhode Island, "whether you are in the dining room or boardroom, knowing what to do, when to do it, and how to do it with polish and style gives you a competitive edge."

In addition to noticing new opportunities for learning good manners, I'm encouraged because the little girl on the commuter train has good company all around her. Even during those days when we experience several instances of boorish behavior, courtesy abounds. People still value "please," "thank you," "may I?" and "excuse me."

Holding the door open for the next person still happens, as does holding a chair for a companion being seated. We hear apologies when people dial our phones mistakenly.

As I exited the commuter train with my memories of the pigtailed paper carrier, I checked my notebook for directions to my appointment. A young man walking alongside offered, "Can I help you? Where are you going?"

For a couple of seconds, I eyed him carefully. I knew I had gone against a well-respected safety precaution. You aren't supposed to look lost in a large city—makes you an easy target for criminals. But this man's concern appeared genuine, so I answered him:

"I'm looking for Peachtree Street, going to the Fulton County Building."

"That's easy," he said, while we climbed the stairs to street level. "You go out the exit door over there, and you'll be on Peachtree. Turn right, and go a block. It's on the corner of Martin Luther King."

"Thanks," I answered. "Thought I had it right. Appreciate your help very much."

Who knows—maybe the next time I think people have quit using courtesy as one of our warmest forms of communication, I'll take another ride on the commuter train.

ASKING FOR ADVICE

YOU MAY HAVE READ HARVEY McKAY'S BOOKS, such as *Swim with the Sharks without Being Eaten Alive.* He's a successful Minneapolis businessman, speaker, and author.

Repeatedly, McKay says his most productive communication activity has been this one—asking advice from people he respects. In his words: "When I got started, I'd use anyone who would listen to me, my banker, my lawyer, my father . . . the fellows I played golf with on Wednesday afternoons. I was shameless in seeking advice. I still am. How can you get hurt asking for an opinion?"

He admits that entrepreneurs have "an instinct to fly solo." Yet, he adds, "Doing so could cut us off from sources of useful advice."

I agree wholeheartedly. Asking for advice ranks among our greatest communication privileges. Calling on the collective wisdom of achievers, we're almost sure to surpass our own solitary judgment.

I've found that most people will share advice when we ask them. The request compliments them, illustrating that we respect their judgment. Also, achievers remember how they climbed the ladder—by seeking sound advice from others. Talking with us offers a chance to return life-changing favors.

In seeking an appointment, ask, "When could I have fifteen minutes to get your advice?" Stating a time limit appeals. Additionally, you've declared the purpose of a meeting. Keep in mind that you'll enjoy second and third appointments by honoring the announced time span for the first one.

When you meet with your advisor, bring a written summary of the subject under consideration. Hand the page to him or her at the outset. Even if neither of you looks at it during your conversation, your host will know you prepared. If you're dealing with an individual who places high value on structure, deliver the summary a couple of days prior to the meeting.

I recommend using specific questions, not generalities. Rather than asking, "Where should I seek a job?" ask, "With my qualifications, do you think I'd be better off in banking or as an account representative with an investment firm?"

Be ready to truly *listen for the advice that's offered.* We're tempted to impress our professional idols by giving our own solutions. Next time you ask for advice, allot only 25 percent of the conversation for your comments.

A final note: When we seek advice, we retain the option to reject it or follow it. Experts make poor choices, just as we do. Regardless of the person's stature, evaluate the counsel carefully before you agree.

Having voiced this precaution, I remain amazed at how often suggestions from others are worth putting into action.

GIVING ADVICE

ONE OF SHAKESPEARE'S MOST ACCLAIMED SCENES has Polonius giving advice to his son Laertes, who was leaving the country. The father's speech included passages which have remained popular. "Neither borrower nor lender be" and "To thine own self be true, and thou canst not then be false to any man" stand out among them.

Possibly our praise for Polonius stems from recognition of how difficult advice giving can be. We admire Polonius for finding the appropriate words for a pivotal point in Laertes' life. We envy Polonius for having a script writer. We don't. We improvise, often with little preparation. Our counsel takes place in real life, not on a stage.

Think back to friends and co-workers who have sought your guidance. They ask: "Can you tell me how to please my mother?" "Should I accept the job offer?" "What's your suggestion on getting along with the new manager?" "How do you think I can move up the ranks quickly?" "Will I be better off working somewhere else?"

How do you answer these inquiries? Our impulse is to become the *relationship repairman.* We listen for three minutes, then give a five-point solution, guaranteed to straighten out a messy situation.

Here, however, our communication impulse is not the course to follow. For one thing, we cannot know *all the facts.* We only know what the person describes, from his or her perspective. Further, the speaker's perspective might be clouded by an inordinate stress level.

Let's suppose we knew all the facts. Even then, issuing a prescription for successful behavior goes beyond the role of an advisor. After all, we're talking about *their life, not ours. They* will face the consequences of recommended actions.

So, what's the suitable response when an individual asks, "What do you think I need to do?"

Carl Rogers spent his lifetime developing what he called "client-centered therapy." As a psychology professor and author, he revolutionized the practice of counseling. His influence works for amateur advisors, too.

Rogers accentuated the importance of the advisor as one who *helps guide another person through the decision-making process*. The advisor *asks the right questions* . . . and encourages the advisee to select the answers.

For a more recent guide to advice giving, I recommend Dr. David Burns' books, especially *Feeling Good: The New Mood Therapy*. Like Rogers, he writes with commendable simplicity.

Using the approaches endorsed by Rogers, Burns, and other respected students of behavior, here's a concise sample of the customary way to give advice, followed by the preferred method.

The Customary Advice-Giver

Advisor: "How can I help you?"

Advisee: "Tell me, should I marry Tim?"

Advisor: "Certainly not. Seems pretty unstable. You'll have a miserable life, I'm sure. Find somebody with a steadier lifestyle."

The Preferred Method

Advisor: "How can I help you?"

Advisee: "Tell me, should I marry Tim?"

Advisor: "It appears you must have some doubts about your relationship. Is that correct?"

Advisee: "Well, yes, I admit I do."

Advisor: "What would be some of the reasons you've become skeptical?"

Advisee: "One of the big problems is . . ."

Clearly, the advisor becomes a *catalyst*—generating a series of questions to assist the advisee in identifying problems. The next step will be to identify possible solutions, weigh the advantages and disadvantages of each, and stimulate the advisee to choose the most beneficial alternative.

Polonius, you see, didn't offer a perfect model for advisors. He issued answers, ignoring questions. Much as we admire the beauty of his speech, I recommend Stephen Covey's suggestion that we deal "with the reality inside another person's head and heart."

THE SWEETEST SOUND

SHORTLY AFTER THE RESTAURANT HOSTESS SEATED Nick and me, the waitress greeted us, gave us her name, and took our orders. About five minutes later she walked past our table.

"Rebecca," I called out, "can you please bring some bread while we wait for our main items?"

She looked shocked. I thought about what I had said, and I couldn't identify anything potentially offensive. Then she took a deep breath and explained.

"Sorry, but you really surprised me. Very few customers catch my name when I tell them. And even if they do, they don't use it. Probably they forget."

"Well, Rebecca, that's interesting. I used your name because I know it's important to you."

She smiled, and was exceptionally helpful throughout the meal.

Rebecca reminded me of a time-honored saying: "There's no sound sweeter to you than the sound of your own name." That's so true. Think back to when you joined a group. You started feeling you belonged *when the members started calling you by name.*

During the years I spent leading fund-raising campaigns, I noticed how meticulous contributors are when charitable organizations list their names publicly. A misspelling evokes wrath. Even leaving out a middle initial prompts phone calls. Certainly the worst error omitted the name entirely. In those cases, the offended parties launched verbal attacks against the clerical staff.

"How," they wondered, "could *anyone* not get my name right?"

We've all met people whose capacity for remembering names borders on miraculous. James A. Ziegler, president of Ziegler Dynamics in Norcross, Georgia, astounds the thousands of people who attend his seminars and speeches annually. Jim will meet up to 150 people when they enter the room, shaking hands, introducing himself, and gazing at their name tags. When the group gets seated, he asks, "Will you please put your hand over your name tag?" Then he goes around the room, *calling out the first names of everyone he has just met!* In smaller training groups with thirty-five attendees, by noon of the first day he'll demonstrate his rare skill by identifying everybody *by first and last names!* As you can guess, his name recognition and recall are marvelous assets, boosting Jim's popularity as a speaker and trainer.

Although the great majority of us can't aspire to his level of expertise with names, we can improve our performance by forming these habits:

When introduced, listen intently. Admittedly, we fail to do that. Why? Because we're focusing on *what we're going to say next.* Going back to the example of Rebecca the waitress, customers miss her name because they are concentrating on their orders. Give the name top priority—because the speaker does!

On hearing the name, visualize it. In Rebecca's case, the task was simple. She wore a name tag. Lacking that advantage, form a mental picture. *See the name in writing.*

In case of an unusual name, ask for the spelling. Inquire about the origin. People will respond warmly to your interest.

Use the person's name in your first response. Right away, you'll wake up your memory. Equally as important, you'll establish rapport.

Associate the name when possible. You hear the name Bruce. Quickly, who else do you know named Bruce? Put these two people together in a mental photo. The task becomes easier when the name carries a natural association. For example, the name Green prompts you to "color" the person.

Ask for a business card, offering your own simultaneously. Luckily, many cards include photos, assisting name recall in the future.

When no cards are available, write the name. No need to be discreet. You'll compliment the individual by demonstrating unusual concern for accuracy and permanence.

I invite you to try my suggestions. Add the ones you find effective. More frequently, you'll be using the sweetest sounds people like to hear.

REFERRALS BECOME DOOR OPENERS

SUPPOSE YOU ARE WANTING TO GET IN TOUCH WITH somebody who can give you a job or buy your product. You have the information you need—name, title, phone number.

Unfortunately, you're suffering "call reluctance."

One reason is, you don't like strangers calling you. Almost always, you tune out the unfamiliar person, ending the conversation soon, though trying to extend courtesy. Since you react to cold calls that way, you're sure the prospects on your list will respond identically . . . or worse.

Happily, a solution to the "cold call fear" exists. You avoid cold calling by having somebody else lay the groundwork for you. The dreaded cold call becomes a "warm call," through the help of a highly credible individual.

Let's say you want to visit a large, national corporation. The traditional method of calling has several likely options, none of them in your favor. The company submerges you into a maze of voice-mail directions; you hear "We're not interested" from a staff person well below the top level; or you're asked to "send your sample materials, and we'll get back with you." Which you do—but they don't.

The referral method requires you to begin by making a list of influential people you know. Review the list with somebody who's familiar with your target company and these people. Ask about *significant relationships*—who serves or served on the board, who went to college with a company official or director, who has ties to your community, who gives the company considerable business, or who has a child working there.

Having identified connections, you'll call to set appointments with the people with clout. Explain, without apology, why you need advice and influence. Describe the project you intend to take to the company. Be specific with your proposal.

Your next step is to say, "How do you think I can see the right person there?" I prefer this tactic to a directive from you. Usually, the caliber of person we're thinking about to help secure an appointment knows how to capitalize on his or her relationship with a colleague.

Typical answers: "I'll call and get an appointment for you." "I'll write a letter introducing you," or "I'll phone the CEO to ask him to see you."

If you are super fortunate, your friend will offer to set up the appointment, and go with you. This represents the ultimate endorsement.

Most likely, you'll follow up a lead on your own. But that's fine. You have a lead to follow!

In making your phone call, *use your referring person's name before you use your own*. They're known and respected there, while you aren't (yet). "Ellen Stewart called you on my behalf yesterday" gets maximum attention.

Referrals work because we're utilizing already-established credibility. It's not ours, but our colleague has allowed us to borrow it.

During one six-month period, I wasted hundreds of telephone hours calling organizations where my name had no recognition or respect. I was systematic, hard working, and spoke with enthusiasm. Doors didn't open. Eventually, friends told me I was using an outmoded approach.

I stopped speaking for myself, letting someone else do that for me. Now my percentage of returned calls, appointments, and eventual business has improved noticeably. Though I still hear my share of "we'll get back to you," "not right now," and "no," I at least get through to decision makers more frequently.

Remember, *referrals open doors you wouldn't even get a glimpse of on your own.*

LET'S NEGOTIATE

MY WIFE, SANDRA, TEACHES SECOND GRADE. ON A daily basis, students come to her yelling about conflicts and heated confrontations. Frequently, two students approach her, with each claiming the other provoked the argument.

"How do you handle those situations?" I asked. "Do you simply make a decision, and tell them who deserves punishment and who has to apologize?"

"Oh, not at all," she told me. "I ask them to leave the classroom, so they can have a couple of minutes to talk and decide what *really* happened. I want them to make the decision, not me."

"Well, does this work?"

"Every time. Not once, in all my years of teaching, have I seen them continue to blame each other entirely. They realize no one person should get all the blame—or walk away guiltless. As they talk, each makes concessions. There's give-and-take."

"You're saying negotiate?"

"Oh, sure. One will admit he pushed the other one, and the second one will confess he said something to anger the student who pushed."

Amazing! Under adult supervision, we learn very early in life how to resolve differences amicably. Events requiring negotiation skills present themselves in all kinds of settings. Teenagers negotiate with their parents on curfews. Spouses negotiate over the purchase price of a home. You negotiate with your boss over a proposed raise. Car dealers anticipate negotiation from customers. Moved to the highest level, countries negotiate economic and territorial disputes, thereby sidestepping war.

Mark McCormack earned fame as the agent who negotiated contracts for super athletes, with golfer Arnold Palmer as his most famous client. McCormack believes you can negotiate almost any variations in opinions and goals. As an example, he says a person who has reserved thirty places for dinner in an upscale restaurant might request a reduction from the menu price, since she is guaranteeing the restaurant so much business for the evening.

One of my graduate-school friends became a champion negotiator, *because he asked.* In fact, he asked in places no one else would consider negotiation sites. He'd enter a shoe store, note the price of a pair he wanted, and tell the salesperson, "Too high." Next, he offered a price 25 percent less than the listed price.

"I can't do that," the employee would say.

"No, but I'll bet your manager can. Go ask him. Tell him I have the money ready. I'll buy at the price I've offered, or leave. He decides." With remarkable frequency, he left after buying the shoes on his terms.

Mark McCormack recommends asking stimulating questions, rather than making dogmatic statements. He counsels us to *"question everything,"* proposing "a healthy skepticism to any rules, numbers, and assumptions in a negotiation."

Experts underscore the value of win-win solutions—no absolute winners, no absolute losers. The shoe store retained a profit, despite the 25 percent reduction. Look at what happens with those second grade students: "They become friends," Sandra says. "They're pleased when arguments change into conciliation."

If I win all I want, and you lose everything, negotiation hasn't happened. *Both of us* should feel we benefit from the communication exchange.

In *The Eight Essential Steps to Conflict Resolution,* Dudley West pulls our thoughts together in writing that conflict does not define a relationship. Rather, conflict "is but one part of a complex and useful relationship."

FOLLOWING THROUGH

AN ATHLETE'S FOLLOW-THROUGH MOTION PROVIDES one of the most graceful sights in sports. Make a mental picture now of the golfer, baseball batter, and tennis player who have contacted the ball, then moved on to a full, well-balanced finish. Or picture the field-goal kicker in football, with foot extended but eyes fixed on the spot where the ball had rested a second ago.

As in sports, following through in communication looks graceful—and helps us to score more effectively.

Kathleen serves as vice president of an important organization, with membership listing in the thousands and a budget in the millions. She's responsible for membership growth. Under her direction, the group has expanded significantly in the last five years.

Another responsibility Kathleen has is arranging training programs. She explained why she selected a certain individual to direct workshops.

"I met him at a reception," she said. "But I meet lots of people in those settings—and remember only a few. During our short conversation, he described an article he had written. I responded positively, expecting nothing beyond our conversation. In cases like this, most people fail to take advantage of the cultivation they've done."

She continued: "A couple of days later, I received the article in the mail, with a note referring to our conversation. This impressed me. He *followed through* with action. He demonstrated that he took our conversation seriously." The result? She hired him to direct two workshops—and told him why she selected him from a large pool of applicants.

Kathleen's advice has value. Following through will set us apart from those who say "I'll call you next week," "Let's go to lunch soon," "We'll talk about this some more"—then fail to communicate again.

Using our comparison to athletics, adopt this slogan: *"While others head for the showers after initial contact, I'm still playing hard and smart."*

CREDIBILITY COUNTS

RALPH WALDO EMERSON LEFT A VIRTUAL TREASURE of wise observations. Among my favorites: "What you are speaks so loudly that I cannot hear a word you say."

Hundreds of years earlier, Aristotle told his students that the orator "must make his own character look right." His statement applies to one-on-one communication as aptly as to public speaking.

Contemporary slang echoes these sages in more common language: "It's not enough to talk the talk—you've gotta walk the walk."

Actor Christopher Reeve illustrates the role of credibility perfectly. Turn back to the mid-1990s, before his paralyzing accident. Suppose he had used his celebrity status to call for greater financial support for spinal injury patients. Because of his fame gained in *Superman, Somewhere in Time,* and other films, he would have generated a degree of interest. Contributions would have come in steadily. Corporations and congressmen would have listened politely, and participated moderately.

We all know what really happened. He spoke with more than words and goodwill. The published and televised photos of him speaking from his huge special chair captivated those who had seen him earlier as an active, athletic person. Understandably, he emerged as the international symbol for paralysis patients.

The public listens to him intently, because Christopher Reeve testifies *through his own experience* what it means to go from good health to immobility in a matter of seconds.

Whenever someone tries to convince us about an idea, inquire about the speaker's *experience with the topic.* The chairperson of a financial campaign requests your gift—has she contributed? How generously?

A politician proclaims, "Vote for me, and you're voting for family values." What's his record as the head of a family?

When we are sending messages, here are basic steps to reinforce our credibility:

Mention your relevant education

Refer to endorsements from respected authorities and acquaintances

Cite experiences which add to your credentials

Let your speech—diction, mannerisms, vocabulary—reflect quality

Display tolerance for the opposition

Express sympathy for another's troubles

Tell about your affiliation with credible organizations

Words, then, start the persuasive cycle. *Who we are* makes the words believable.

WHY WE SAY THOSE CRAZY THINGS

"HERE'S LOOKING AT *YOU*, KID." WHO MADE THOSE words famous? Practically any movie fan will answer correctly, naming Humphrey Bogart as the speaker and Ingrid Bergman as the listener in the film *Casablanca*.

Other expressions came to us from movies. "Go ahead, make my day" calls to mind Clint Eastwood as "Dirty Harry" Callahan.

Television creates sayings which we incorporate into our everyday speech. "Been there, done that" appeared on the screen before adorning shirts and bumper stickers. When *Laugh In* skyrocketed to the top in the 1960s, dozens of the show's signature lines hit the streets, ranging from "Very interesting"(spoken slowly, accenting every syllable), to "Sock it to me!" to "I didn't know that!" (uttered with alarming bewilderment).

Novels contribute idioms, too. When we complain, "I'm in a catch-22 situation," we're referring, maybe unknowingly, to Joseph Heller's novel *Catch 22*. The book depicted life at a World War II air base. The rule book included number twenty-two, stipulating that fighter pilots could leave the base only under two conditions: death or insanity. Death wasn't a desirable excuse. Yet those who chose the route of declaring insanity would prove by their wise choice that they were sane! Ever since, when we feel trapped by impossible rules, we borrow the novel's title.

We're not sure where some of our most-used expressions originated. Was it penmanship teachers who coined "Mind your p's and q's," advising students to know which side of a circle gets the mark for those two letters? A more colorful account takes us to bar scenes, where bartenders let "p's" indicate pints and "q's" indicate quarts. When a patron had consumed enough ale to risk becoming a nuisance, the bartender would issue this warning.

Historical incidents leave language trails. "His name is mud" goes back to Lincoln's assassination by John Wilkes Booth. Booth broke his leg in a jump from the balcony to the stage of Ford's Theater. Escaping, he found Dr. Charles Mudd nearby. Although Dr. Mudd didn't know about Booth's involvement in the slaying, government officials railroaded him into prison for treating Booth. Thus "His name is mud" (note the shortened spelling for the last name) became a judgment for anyone who fell into public disgrace.

Speaking of mud, "Here's mud in your eye" grew into a popular toast after World War I. English and American soldiers, covered by battlefield dirt, hoisted their glasses and wished each other well while recognizing their splattered condition.

For those interested in reading about the origin of other slang expressions, I recommend Lawrence Urdang's delightful little volume, *The Whole Ball of Wax and Other Colloquial Phrases*.

Knowing how phrases appear cautions us to be careful about the cute remark we make today. Maybe it's so cute it will become tomorrow's cliché.

2

NONVERBAL COMMUNICATION

OUR EVERYDAY LANGUAGE REVEALS OUR HEAVY dependence on physical references for expressing ourselves. Consider "keep your chin up," "turning a cold shoulder," "stiff upper lip," "down in the mouth," "turned her nose up at him," "turned his back on me," "looked the other way," "turned a deaf ear," "went into this with her eyes wide open," "a leg up on the competition," "foot in the door," "put his foot in his mouth," "tight fisted"—we could continue almost endlessly! We have hundreds of expressions which speak volumes, just by depicting nonverbal activities.

Increasing our understanding of nonverbal communication principles will assist us in sending messages. We want to *look like* what we're saying.

Conversely, these principles enable us to add another dimension to interpreting messages from others.

Researchers have not reached full agreement on the percentage of being understood which results from nonverbal cues. Estimates range from 30 percent to 70 percent. All agree that their impact is very substantial. The complete communicator acts accordingly.

MESSAGES SENT BY OUR TIME MANAGEMENT

THE COLLEGE I WAS SERVING AS A VICE PRESIDENT was interviewing candidates for a consulting job. The two finalists displayed solid credentials, and impressed us with their speaking skills. However, their nonverbal behavior—particularly their time management—detracted from their professionalism.

We scheduled the first candidate to meet with me and the president in the president's office at 11:00 A.M. We waited five minutes. We waited fifteen. At the twenty-minute mark, the consultant called to say, "I'm about forty-five minutes away from you. See you when I get there."

When he arrived, he offered no apologies. Not surprisingly, we hired the other candidate.

On the new hire's first day on campus, he interviewed five people. Sounds all right, but he was supposed to interview ten. Apparently, he never checked his watch during interviews. He obliterated our carefully structured schedule. The result? The people who met with him grew tired of listening past the appointed time, and he infuriated those who expected to see him, but didn't.

Through his tardiness, the first interviewed candidate communicated, "Your time isn't valuable, so I can arrive whenever I want to."

By ignoring the schedule for faculty and staff interviews, the consultant we hired communicated, "These people are lucky to have me talk with them—and I'll talk at length to those I enjoy, then skip the others."

Likewise, the employee who arrives late for work, can't finish jobs on schedule, and leaves the job early conveys an attitude an employer won't reward—and won't tolerate indefinitely.

On a more positive note, people who manage their time effectively communicate that they can manage themselves and their responsibilities. Also, they communicate their respect for others.

What do you tell people (without speaking) about your management of time? Do they sense that you are highly professional and reliable?

Be sure to honor the clock and the calendar. Speaking personally, I show up for appointments at least ten minutes early. My promptness suggests: "I'm ready, even eager to see you. Our meeting holds high priority for me." Not once have I considered those ten minutes "wasted" time. Before speaking a word, I signal strong interest.

From a pragmatic viewpoint: your promotions and raises are more likely to come on time—if *you're* on time.

I WONDER WHAT SHE MEANT BY THAT

THE LAST TIME YOU WENT GROCERY SHOPPING, DID you notice anything unusual about the clerks—either those who roamed the aisles or those who ran the cash registers? Did they look at you as you drew near? Did they smile? If they looked at you and smiled, would you consider their friendliness one of their job responsibilities?

I ask the question because of a complaint filed by twelve Safeway employees. With almost fourteen hundred stores, Safeway operates the second largest supermarket chain in the nation.

The complaint arose because Safeway began enforcing a rule requiring employees to make eye contact with and smile at customers the minute they walk into conversational range. Do you see any problem with the rule?

Safeway employees did, because their direct gazes and warm smiles led to distorted interpretations. Male customers mistook the nonverbal behavior as an invitation to intimacy. A produce clerk reported daily aggression from customers who thought she was flirting with them. A co-worker talked of hiding in the back room to avoid overzealous males—some of whom followed her to her car and propositioned her.

A San Francisco male customer told reporters he had grown accustomed to the friendliness, which he considered nothing more than a job-related duty. In his opinion, "You'd have to be very narcissistic or stupid to believe that the flattery was personally directed at you."

The Safeway story reminds us that nonverbal actions are likely to foster more than one interpretation, including some which are far removed from reality.

You're talking with someone, and the listener folds her arms. Judging by the magazine articles you've read, she has moved into a "closed" position. She's defending herself. She's rejecting you.

Well, while those interpretations represent possible reasons for her arm position, let's realize she could be folding her arms because the room is cold, and she reflexively seeks warmth this way. Or the position might stem from a longtime habit, which she isn't aware of. Or she's tired, and finds the position relaxing.

A student chooses a front-row seat in every classroom. Is this the student with the highest level of interest? Maybe, maybe not. One student goes there to see more clearly, another one to hear better, another one to shut out distractions of students in rows ahead. Or, yes, another student has strong intellectual curiosity. Who knows why she sits there? Probably couldn't explain it herself.

One man with a very dour—almost sour—facial expression confided to a friend: "You know, people consider me glum and unfriendly. They think I'm a scowler. I try to assure them I don't mean anything by my demeanor, because I'm not aware of a sullen expression. Even my mother used to tell me I needed to work on the perception I'm creating."

You're talking with a co-worker. He stretches, then yawns widely. Aha—you're boring him! Once more, maybe and maybe not. He might be so sleep-deprived that he yawns from weariness.

Here's my word of caution. Too many books and articles have created self-appointed experts who see an individual's posture, gestures, distance from a conversation partner, facial expression—and they profess, "I'll tell you *exactly* what that guy is thinking."

These "experts" have gone too far. Nonverbal cues become clues, yes—but they're not infallible. Just ask the Safeway clerks who offered their bright smiles merely to please their employer and found themselves being misunderstood.

WHAT DOES YOUR BUSINESS LOOK LIKE?

THINK ABOUT THE TIMES YOU HAVE GONE HOUSE hunting. You selected houses you wanted to walk through, and eliminated others. Usually, your decision was spontaneous.

"But I like that place. Why don't we stop and take a tour?" one family member says, while another remarks—with an equally strong opinion—"No, it just doesn't look right."

"Well, what don't you like about it?"

"Can't really say. I just know we'd waste time stopping here."

Prospective customers look at our places of business the same way. When they see the facility, some will keep driving (or even speed up), others will tap the brakes lightly, and—thankfully—some will stop and enter.

Carl Sewell, who sells luxury cars in Dallas, Texas, wrote an excellent book on customer service, *Customers for Life*. Repeatedly, Sewell talks about what appearances communicate to prospective buyers. When he decided the city's street sweeper did an inadequate job in front of his auto dealership, he bought his own equipment. Also, he spent far more than most dealers would spend on wallpaper for customer restrooms. Selling first-class cars, he didn't think he should offer second-class surroundings.

For two years, I conducted fund-raising campaigns for a college whose buildings and grounds suffered from deferred maintenance. Inside, the buildings were dark and gloomy. The exteriors needed paint, roofing, and window replacement. Even though the college enjoyed a fine academic reputation and a respected tradition, alumni and friends said the institution did not *look like a winner.* Frequently I heard, "Giving to your college seems like pouring money down a rat hole."

A few months before I started writing this book, Atlanta hosted a professional golf tournament. Greens keepers groomed the course to perfection. Despite tornado damage a few days before the first round, players spoke favorably about course conditions.

However, what did spectators comment on most? Numerous letters to the editor complained about distant parking lots and infrequent shuttle buses. Rolling hills, tall pines, pristine fairways, and a gorgeous clubhouse could not compensate for faulty transportation. Apparently, fans interpreted the transportation snafus this way: "We don't care where you have to park, or how far you walk afterward."

Let's be sure that our place of business, both outdoors and indoors, sends a more hospitable message—one like, "Come on in, we've put down the red carpet."

Do that, and you'll enjoy the crowds that keep on coming.

CASUAL DRESS—ARE YOU SERIOUS?

FOR SEVERAL YEARS, EMPLOYEES AND MANAGERS have talked about "dressing for success." The term became popular with publication of a book by that title. Ultimately, author John Molloy wrote sequels and spinoffs, repeating the phrase in various ways.

Surely we're all aware of how "successful dress" customs have changed. Pull out college yearbooks from the 1950s and 1960s. Flip to the sports section. You'll see that spectators at football games wore their finest apparel—hats and heels for women, coats and ties (and sometimes hats) for men.

Or remember when you started flying commercially. You'd adorn yourself with the best suit, the most expensive dress. Maybe you bought new clothes for the flight.

Compare those customs with today's. Attend a warm-weather football game, and many of the fans are wearing shorts and visors. As you board a flight, the only ties you'll see are on the pilots. Passengers headed for a beach vacation won't have to change clothes upon landing.

As a reflection of these changes in recreational style, the workplace allows "business casual dress." However, definitions remain vague. What may seem casual to an employee could look sloppy to the employer, co-workers, and customers. To end the confusion, every workplace needs a specific list of what's condoned, and what isn't.

Not long ago I directed a workshop for secretaries, receptionists, and administrative assistants. When we discussed acceptable attire, one woman said: "I've been in the work force for thirty-one years. I've watched the styles move from suits to slacks to shorts. I thought I could get used to the new atmosphere, but I can't. So I'm going to leave my job, and find one where managers respect traditional style and grooming."

Another woman said her husband had ended his job search by signing up with a company where the standard of professional dress seemed quite high. He rejected a bigger salary offer from another company—because he thought that firm's informal dress code symbolized a half-hearted work ethic.

I liked this comment from a participant: "Don't dress for the job you have now," she advised. "Dress for the job you want next."

Several workshop participants said that dressing in nice outfits makes them feel more serious about their work.

One of my former teaching colleagues at the University of Georgia, Dr. Dale Leathers, chose a novel way to impress his students about the impact of clothing. "I walked into one of my classes dressed in a bathrobe and tennis shoes," he reported. "I was wearing sunglasses and smoking a long, black cigar." He began his remarks by asserting that "appearance communicates meaning." Not surprisingly, the students who had grown accustomed to seeing him in more professorial attire "became rather disoriented."

Apparently, despite our cries for relaxed dress codes, *we aren't accepting business casual very casually.*

OLD CLOTHES SEND MESSAGES, TOO

IN THE ARTICLES AND BOOKS DISCUSSING HOW clothing sends a message, invariably the studies focus on contemporary clothing—what we're wearing currently. I believe there's a serious omission here. Clothing from our past says plenty, too.

Take a mental hike to a typical attic. You'd find items like these:

A wedding dress. Maybe the dress has hung there for thirty years, surrounded by protective covering, yet visible. The woman who wore the dress doesn't anticipate a second show. She bought the dress for one-time use only.

Nor does she want a relative to wear the dress, unless a daughter makes a sentimental plea for the special privilege.

Nobody would buy the dress. Even if they would, she wouldn't sell.

A football jersey, blue with a gold number 11. The player's last name appears above the number.

The jersey belongs to the son, whose football days ended when he left high school. Here again, the article of clothing is not kept to wear. Actually, the quarterback now looks more like a tackle, several sizes away from his playing days.

The jersey hangs there as a reminder of rivalries, home-coming games, Friday-night hysteria, and forty-eight minutes of family unity each week.

An old fishing hat. Her father wore the hat, usually on Wednesday afternoons when the stores closed in the little town. No guessing how many times this hat endured rain, perspiration, and searing sunshine. Whenever she sees the hat, she pictures the fisherman returning.

"How'd it go?" she asked as he got out of the pickup truck.

"Not bad. Take a look at these!" He opened the pail as he came through the back porch, depositing his hat on the shelf, where he'd retrieve it the next Wednesday.

She thought back to the day of her father's funeral.

"That was tough, of course. The next day was just as sorrowful, when we went through his clothes, so we could discard some and give some to the needy. You can see, though, I couldn't give his old hat to anybody. *He's with me* when I see this misshapen, faded head cover."

Yes, our attics and closets reveal who we are, by revealing who we have been.

KEEPING THE VERBAL AND NONVERBAL MESSAGES CONSISTENT

IMAGINE YOURSELF MEETING WITH YOUR NEW supervisor for the first time.

You walk in, the supervisor remains seated. You say hello, and she barely looks up as she continues to shuffle papers. She motions you to a chair twenty feet away from her desk.

Skipping personal remarks entirely, she hands you a written assignment. While you read, she takes a phone call and talks for five minutes. When the call ends, she rises without apology to signal your dismissal.

On your way out, she says, "You can feel free to call on me anytime. My door is always open. I'm available to help with any job you're handling. Oh, another thing . . . I really value your opinions and suggestions."

You leave surrounded by a cloud of confusion. The manager promised availability and partnership—but acted like a robot who thinks of you as a hired hand.

What's the problem?

The problem is a conflicting set of messages. We call this *incongruent communication.* The words sounded supportive and warm. Yet the behavior was cold, distant, reserved.

Think of how different you'd feel if the supervisor had greeted you at the door with a handshake, ushered you to a chair next to hers in front of the desk, given instructions to hold her phone calls, smiled warmly, and maintained steady eye contact.

Whatever the communication purpose and setting, it's important for our nonverbal behavior to harmonize with our words. When somebody enters your workplace or home, keep in mind that you'll transmit two sets of messages. Be sure they say the same thing.

WHAT IF SOMEBODY TURNED OFF YOUR SOUND?

ROGER AILES SERVED BOTH PRESIDENT BUSH AND President Reagan as their voice coach. Later, he traveled the nation for a major broadcasting company. His job was to evaluate television talk-show hosts.

In his book *You Are the Message,* Ailes describes his unique method for rating the television personalities. Before he would meet the host or attend a broadcast, Ailes checked into a hotel room. He tuned in to the talk show, and watched the host . . . *with the sound off.*

Ailes watched the host for five or ten minutes, keeping the set silent. If he didn't see anything that made him want to turn the sound on, he'd recommend a replacement for the host.

His next career step involved training corporate speakers. He used the same test. And Ailes recommends evaluating yourself this way. Have a friend, colleague, or family member videotape you at close range. You can be talking with one person, with several, or giving a speech. Any format works, as long as there's ample opportunity to check your expressions and movements.

"Watch yourself," Ailes teaches. "Do your eyes and face look engaged and lively? Do you gesture when you speak? Do you ever smile?"

He notes: "People who are the best communicators communicate with their whole being. They're animated, expressive, interesting to watch."

I endorse his advice. Arrange to see yourself as others see you in a communication activity. As you watch the silent play-back, ask, "Is this person so interesting that I would turn up the volume?"

Here's something I learned from the camcorder—most of us will benefit by *exaggerating our customary movements and expressions*. Few of us err on the side of too much activity. Try increasing your mobility during one of these simulated sessions. Then you'll remain lively, even if somebody were able to turn off your sound.

SYMBOLS SAY PLENTY

WHEN TELEVISION FIRST HIT THE AMERICAN scene, people would stare for hours, hoping to get even a glimpse of a picture. Most of the time viewers saw "snow," similar to what comes onto the screen when the cable system quits during a storm.

In my hometown of Columbia, Mississippi, only one store displayed a television set. Daily, a crowd gathered to fix their eyes on a blurry screen. Some spectators were lucky enough to stand there at the right time. They'd see a shadowy profile moving. "There he is! Look!" We laughed excitedly, patting each other on the back, as though we had accomplished something.

As the product improved, you got the impression that almost every family owned a set. You could see the tall antennae above most rooftops.

However, years later we discovered that manufacturers sold more antennae than TV sets. Why? Well, people who couldn't afford a set wanted others to think they owned a set.

Television ownership represented a certain level of financial achievement. Buyers thought of antennae as symbols conveying favorable impressions.

Sound silly, almost absurd? Actually, symbols have played important roles in nonverbal communication in every culture we're familiar with. Nations have gone to war to protect what symbols stand for—Old Glory, the swastika, the rising sun, the Cross come to mind instantly.

Commercially, symbols identify, publicize, and even become synonymous with world-famous products. Spot a golden arch on the side of the highway, and you don't need to see the name of the restaurant you're approaching.

When I have an appointment with someone for the first time, I feel fortunate when an assistant ushers me into the person's office, and I wait there instead of a reception area. In the office, I browse the symbols quickly. *Symbols tell me what this person values.*

On the shelves surrounding me, I might see golf trophies, artifacts from other countries, family photographs, citations from civic organizations, a shovel used for ground breaking, a photograph with a celebrity (usually autographed), favorite books, diplomas, a gavel signifying club presidency, a football autographed by a coach—you've seen these, and numerous other symbols.

Think about your advantage. In three minutes of looking (you're not prying, because the person displays these items proudly for everyone to admire), you have had this individual give a biographical sketch . . . *without uttering a single word.*

The executive comes in, greets you, and waits for your opening. Pointing to a trophy, you comment, "Looks like you're an avid golfer." That's just *one* choice among many the person gave you.

Shift the focus to yourself. Which symbols say something about you? I know an insurance salesman whose company told him to trade in his rather ancient car. The district manager informed him, "You're trying to save money, I see. However, you're losing money. Prospects who look at your car will assume you haven't had much success in selling. They'll wonder why. Upgrade your auto, and more people will want to be with you because you *look like have been selling.*"

Entering a meeting, bring your pad and pen. Your nonverbal message: "I'm sure the information shared here is going to be worth keeping."

I've become aware of consultants who specialize in helping clients select stationery which harmonizes with the company's message. Jackie Howard, owner of Paces Paper in the Buckhead section of Atlanta, claims: "Paper is how people see you when you're not there."

Naturally, we want our business cards to reflect our mission without confusion. A trend I've noticed: more photos appearing on cards. Photos turn the card from print to a person—one who's right there, ready to help.

In every communication effort, observe what others say through their symbols. On your part, present symbols which say *what you want to say about yourself.*

MY SPACE OR YOURS?

DURING HIS LIFETIME, DR. DALE LEATHERS established an international reputation as an expert on nonverbal communication. In *Successful Nonverbal Communication: Principles and Applications,* he wrote: "The way we use space clearly communicates meaning. . . . The beliefs, the values, and, ultimately, the meaning of a culture are communicated by the way people handle space."

An administrator told me, "I have had to handle every imaginable sort of crisis as a manager. But nothing brings more hostility than an effort to change an employee's office location or parking space."

A college official drew unexpected wrath from an occupant of a building next door when he asked for a reserved parking space in the adjacent lot. The occupant wrote the president, accusing the offender of "commandeering the lot."

Dr. Leathers calls our spatial behavior "proxemics." Obviously, the term relates to what is proximate, or nearby.

People become connected with their habitual space. After long association, they feel violated when circumstances threaten their monopoly.

Consider these commonplace examples:

> You go to a civic club for the first time. Seeing an empty chair, you sit and introduce yourself. The seven people at the table greet you, but you feel a chill in their tone. Soon a gentleman arrives, looks at you, turns without a word, and leaves. After the meeting, a friend informs you that the man who left had been sitting in that chair each Tuesday for the last ten years.

> Next time, you'll sit elsewhere.

> The same can happen in houses of worship. Families have "their pew." Even if they arrive late, they expect to have the place available. A visitor risks chaotic embarrassment by seating his family there.

> At home, family members don't wonder where *their places* are. To verify how ingrained our territoriality is, try taking another family member's chair, either at the dining table or in the television room. You won't stay there long. You can't get away with *invading space* that others have claimed.

> Note: the civic club, the church, the family don't have signs marked RESERVED. No need for a sign. By custom, the tables and pews and easy chairs *are* reserved.

We live in a highly mobile society. Relocating to another city creates instant disorientation. Now you have no places to claim. And as you seek space, what are the rules? Whose territory will you disrespect quite innocently? A nomadic family won't say, "We're well settled in our new city" until each person has secured personal space.

The more we understand proxemics, the more we'll respect people's innate sense of ownership for the physical niches where we work and live.

Note some of the possible changes we'll make:

We'll make no more "drop in ('cold') calls," because unscheduled visits take us across territorial lines without an invitation.

We'll make our work space appear accessible and inviting, dropping old barriers erected to declare our sole sovereignty. I could show you a hospital public relations office whose entrance door stays shut. I picture a wide moat with no bridge. An open door would indicate, "We really *are* interested in relating to the public."

We'll prepare presentations with the receiver's *spatial allegiances* in mind. Maybe we've had the habit of placing papers on a supervisor's desk when we came in for a meeting. From now on, we'll keep them in our hands or notebook.

3

WRITING

WILLIAM FAULKNER SAID ABOUT WRITING, "WHEN you've finished, you hope that it is expressed so that everyone can understand it and derive some benefit from it."

What a concise, powerful clarification of the purpose of writing—to bring understanding and benefit to readers! You may want to consider keeping a copy of those words near your computer, typewriter, or pen and paper.

Notice I didn't say *creative writing*. I consider the phrase redundant, for unless you're copying someone else's work, *all writing is creative*. Yes, I'm including routine memos, e-mails, minutes of meetings, letters to friends and relatives, articles for the newspaper, book manuscripts, poetry—whatever your writing task, creativity reigns supreme.

I applaud writing teachers and those who publish magazines and books about writing. Their advice is valuable, used judiciously. Nevertheless, I caution against looking for a "formula" for clear, persuasive writing. No formula works for everybody.

I hope this chapter gives you, as Faulkner would say, something you understand and can use.

Forget Originality, Go for Reality

MANY WOULD-BE WRITERS NEVER PICK UP THE PEN because of a mistaken notion. They assume that authors have to introduce new and striking material.

Here's a surprise for them: originality takes second place in priorities. First place goes to giving an accurate view of the human condition. Put another way, we don't expect writers to offer a window to the future—but we do ask them for mirrors which reflect life as we know it.

Andy Rooney, known both to reading and television audiences, observes: "Writers don't often say anything that readers don't already know, unless it's a news story." He continues, "A writer's greatest pleasure is revealing to people things they knew but did not know that they knew."

If Rooney sounds a bit garbled, he clarifies his counsel by adding: "This produces a warm sense of fellow feeling and is the best a writer can do."

For a classical example, think about Shakespeare. Certainly he wasn't the first person to write about family problems, intrigue, jealousy, thoughts of suicide, insanity, and murder to gain a lover. So what's his claim to greatness?

The answer is that he wrote about human frailty with such exquisite language, and with such penetrating insight, readers and audiences saw their problems differently, and understood themselves better.

Accordingly, Rooney's statement comforts me and you and all aspiring writers. We don't have to create *avant-garde* literature—just a fresh vantage point for what people know already. As Rooney says, this sparks a "sense of fellow feeling."

Writers Are Readers

WE'RE NOT TALKING ABOUT COINCIDENCE WHEN we observe that one of the most productive writers of all time was one of the most insatiable readers. James Michener wrote more than thirty books—most of which belong to the epics category because of their length and the breadth of research behind them.

Michener astounded readers and publishers because he was a one-person research team. "I was interested in everything," he said about his youth. "I was a kind of intellectual vacuum cleaner." He said he mastered at least five hundred books for every major topic he covered. By the age of twenty-four, he thought he had read most of the good novels ever written.

For another testimonial, turn to Larry L. King—not be to confused with the television talk-show host. The King I'll quote has written novels, numerous magazine articles, and the acclaimed musical, *The Best Little Whorehouse in Texas.* Teaching at Princeton, he voiced alarm over "how little my writing students read outside their classroom requirements." King wondered: "What makes them think of a *writing career* if they read neither the old masters nor contemporary writers?" In his customarily acerbic style, King declared: "The writer who fails to read—widely, incessantly, compulsively—is a fool."

Reading opens the door to vital information. Published writers have to write about *something* . . . not just their own ideas thought up on a coffee break.

Reading forms a nesting ground for ideas. Tradition has Sir Isaac Newton saying, "If I have seen farther than other men, it is because I stood on the shoulders of giants." Most geniuses accumulate the brilliance which preceded them, through comprehensive reading.

Reading introduces the seeker to how the finest writers wield their artistry. We live and breathe their style, their wizardry with words, their kaleidoscopic sentences, their character portrayals.

Reading expands our vocabulary, more powerfully than studying a dictionary or thesaurus.

Reading helps fashion our philosophy for living—and the writer must be sure of his vantage point before attempting to share thoughts with others.

In short, the writer cannot draw water from a dry well. The writer replenishes the well through reading, until writing comes from the overflow.

What does the writer read? Like Michener, be "interested in everything." Consider yourself an intellectual sponge.

Granted, the Internet has shifted attention from libraries and bookstores. For my part, I'm ecstatic about the information "Net Search" locates for me in less than five seconds. Let's keep in mind, though, we're talking primarily about excerpts, summaries, reviews, and—thankfully—instant bibliographies.

Much as I rely upon the Internet, I remain optimistic about the place of books in our ongoing personal and professional education. In my judgment, tomorrow's leading writers will be the intellectual pioneers who adore books today.

GOVERNMENT LINGO—HOW NOT TO WRITE

VICE PRESIDENTS DON'T MAKE HEADLINES OFTEN. That's the way it's supposed to be. Some of them bide their time quietly, then run for the top job. Others pass their term, then fade into private life unnoticed.

Once, however, Vice President Al Gore became an exception, capturing front-page attention in most major newspapers. He announced that the federal government would require all employees to use "plain English." President Clinton shared the publicity, saying the call for clarity was intended "to help citizens understand what the government is doing, what it requires, and what services it offers."

You'll join me in applauding that declaration, won't you?

Your experiences may include reading items such as: state and federal tax forms, homestead exemption tax instructions, legislation being proposed, the *Congressional Record*, political position papers, and general regulations.

Speaking of regulations, I'll never forget (though I'd like to) two years I spent as a full-time writer of grant proposals. This responsibility forced me to read the *Federal Register*, a lifeless publication which prints the regulations handed down from various federal agencies. To write an acceptable proposal, you have to muddle through the most incomprehensible word assemblage this side of a physics textbook.

Every time an issue arrived, I dreaded turning to the first page. Too bad Gore's support for ordinary English didn't happen before I took that job.

Gore offered examples of the new government language. Writers will say "exit routes" instead of the cumbersome "means of egress." The new government writing, he assured the public, demands shorter sentences, simple pronouns—"you" in place of "party of the first part"—and elimination of meaningless technical terms.

A decade after the implementation of this new policy, we'll learn whether *governmentese* has disappeared . . . although we can't expect the *Federal Register* to rival *Reader's Digest* for readability.

Whatever the result, the announcement brought relief. Until then, I thought there were people who actually understood Washington's avalanche of gibberish.

SIMPLICITY IMPROVES READABILITY

IN 1992, NOVELIST JAMES MICHENER WROTE HIS memoir, *The World Is My Home.* I bought the book to learn what one of the world's most prolific and brilliant authors revealed about the craft of writing from his vantage point.

He made one recommendation in two words: *write simply.* He explained: "I try to follow the pattern of Ernest Hemingway, who achieved a striking style with short, familiar words."

A superlative scholar throughout his life, Michener acquired a large vocabulary—"but I never had a desire to display it," he observed. He continued, "Good writing . . . consists of trying to use ordinary words to achieve extraordinary results."

Remember those vocabulary lists you memorized, possibly as a college freshman? And how many course advertisements have invited you to "build a stronger vocabulary, so you will impress people"? Books promise "a more powerful vocabulary in thirty days."

On this point, Michener tells about Somerset Maugham, a revered novelist whose career ended as Michener's began. Maugham said he started a notebook when he decided to become a writer. He jotted down words with nice sounds. Years later, he reviewed his list, and realized he had never used a single word from his collection.

Increasing your vocabulary helps you understand the language, because you identify word origins and the relationships among words. As a writer, you increase the number of words at your disposal, allowing you to say the same thing without tiresome repetition. As a reader, you'll comprehend articles and books more easily. Yes, "learn a new word every day" strikes me as a fine habit.

Still, I caution you to hear Michener again: "No writer has to use all the words he does know."

Early in our careers, we were tempted (and often succumbed) to parade our word mastery. In those first job applications, we relied on a thesaurus (a book of words, with several acceptable options for each word) to flaunt our familiarity with such words as "matriculated" rather than enrolled, "perused" rather than read, or "vita" in place of résumé.

Later, when we became supervisors and read job applications and cover letters, we changed our minds. Simple language, we discovered, creates a favorable impression, but pompous language offends readers.

James J. Kilpatrick, a syndicated columnist and respected writing instructor, agrees with Michener. "What is a fundamental principle of writing?" he asks. "It is to convey a message." Kilpatrick says the writer's art "lies in stringing the right words together artfully." By artfully, he means without showing off.

To assure simplicity, write your first draft, review it, and mark through the pretentious words and phrases. Look for more common words. Almost always, they're available.

Mark this down: *Words are not exhibits, they are tools for sending messages our readers will understand and act upon.*

WHY FOREIGN LANGUAGES AREN'T FOREIGN

WORDS FOR WRITERS ARE LIKE BRICKS FOR BRICK masons, brushes for artists, golf clubs for the touring professional—tools to get the job done. Whether you're writing letters, memos, sales proposals, annual reports, a speech for the stockholders' meeting, a novel, or an article for your professional magazine, you are no better than your command of language.

Browse the reference shelf in a quality bookstore, and you'll find numerous books about improving language skills. Often they contain good advice. Experts guarantee we'll increase our vocabulary by learning a few words a week. They recommend working crossword puzzles, keeping a writing journal, and reading widely, both in the classics and contemporary literature.

Maybe you've taken those steps. I commend you. No doubt, your writing showed improvement.

From my experience, I want to offer a seldom-spoken suggestion: *learn at least one language other than your own.* Pay your dues with language study, and you'll have a more versatile arsenal of functional tools.

During my formal education, I was fortunate enough to study four languages other than English. I took Spanish in high school, Greek in college, then French and German in graduate school. Those courses brought me great pleasure. In a way, each one represented a huge puzzle. The challenge was to fit the pieces—in this case, the words—in the right places.

I'm sure these courses helped me as much as the more traditional curriculum—memorizing English vocabulary lists, reading Shakespeare, writing term papers, diagramming sentences (will I ever forget those agonizing assignments?), and similar time-honored pathways to English proficiency.

Other languages helped me understand the derivation of English words. For example, politics related to the Greek word *polis*, meaning city. In fact, knowing foreign languages boosts your vocabulary immensely. You can decipher unfamiliar English words by spotting their roots in other tongues.

Second, learning another country's language helps us understand the nuances of the culture. Logically, you won't be able to write about a culture convincingly until you understand the subtleties. As a resident of the southern part of the United States, I know an exchange student who visits me in Georgia will be lost until he becomes aware of the various meanings of the brief saying "y'all." So it goes elsewhere— learn the idioms, learn the language, learn the customs and culture. *Then* write with authority and credibility.

Third, Americans use a number of foreign terms without explaining them. They assume we know them. When you hear *quid pro quo,* you can contribute to the conversation intelligently when you translate the phrase as "something for something"— something is given or said or done with the expectation of an equivalent response. When a person refers to her *raison d'etre,* and you translate to "reason for being," you're aware the individual is telling you about the central theme of her life.

So count me among those who want to keep, even increase, language requirements at all educational levels. Especially, I repeat, for writers and writers-to-be.

CHANGING THE RULES

THINKING BACK TO SOME OF THE FIRST RULES I heard about writing, naturally I remember my eighth-grade teacher, Miss Blackwell. Miss Blackwell, as we called her with both affection and fear, introduced us to essays, poetry, sentence structure, and the revered rules for writing.

At that age, I joined my classmates in thinking everything she said was correct, and would remain correct forever. In essence, we honored her pronouncements as *Blackwell's Laws.* Our malleable minds didn't ask her to document her commandments for acceptable writing. *She* was sufficient authority herself.

Many years later, I've spent considerable time wondering what Miss Blackwell would say about the expanded latitudes today's writers enjoy. "Miss Blackwell," our class would delight in telling her, "we're allowed to end sentences with prepositions now. You wouldn't allow that. Today's readers and editors will."

Winston Churchill helped break the pattern. When challenged about ending one of his sentences with a preposition, he referred to the time-honored rule this way: "That is foolishness up with which I will not put."

Miss Blackwell would notice, too, that today's writers use incomplete sentences. Like this one. Like this one, too. I shudder when I envision her volatile eruption. Her red pen would demolish those partial sentences. Scribbled across the page: "How can subject and verb agree when there is no verb?" Let me add that thinking about her red pen (her supply room must have kept dozens of them handy) brings me great physical discomfort.

Miss Blackwell wouldn't approve of my punctuation habits. I punctuate without remembering, much less adhering to, the complex rules she hammered into our brains. I use punctuation to foster easier reading. "Bill," she might address me, "identify the independent and dependent clauses on this page. Tell me the comma rules when each is present."

Miss Blackwell, I use one-sentence paragraphs, rather frequently.

"Not possible," she'd proclaim. "Every paragraph, you see, has a *theme sentence* to open the paragraph, then other explanatory/supportive sentences afterward."

"You taught that, yes," I'd remark, "but there's more freedom of style now."

Even as she tried to absorb such shocking news, I add: "And I begin sentences with conjunctions, against your instruction." At this point, I imagine her leaving the classroom, confused and somewhat dizzy.

But (another sentence beginning with a conjunction), my predictions about her might be totally unfair. Really, she might shock me with her progressive opinions. After all, she believed in language use that conveys clear meaning and produces intended responses.

She might express relief. "Well," she could say, "it's about time those rule makers lifted some of the traditional shackles to creativity. At times I wanted to recommend adjustments. I felt, though, no one was ready for revolutionized language."

Ah, yes, Miss Blackwell. As committed as you were to quality education, I'll bet you'd adjust to today's eighth grade curriculum, and inspire contemporary students as commendably as you inspired my class.

MODELS FOR WRITING

WE LEARN TO WALK, TALK, PRACTICE GOOD manners, throw a baseball, or crotchet by watching other people do those things well. Good models show us how to do the task.

Think back to your last trip to the bookstore. As you browsed the shelves, how did you select the books you wanted to browse? I'm sure you looked closely at the covers, especially the book's spine—the part you'll see when the book stands upright, surrounded by other books.

Whether you're writing for a book, newsletter, e-mail, brochure, or your business card, give plenty of attention to format. Several publications stand out as models and "must-reads." No, I'm not referring to books or magazines about writing, but to items available for the general public.

First on my list is *USA Today*, ranking second to *The Wall Street Journal* in national circulation. Count me among *USA Today's* big fans.

I like the format. People who claim packaging doesn't count ought to compare this paper with more traditional ones. *USA Today* displays bright colors, the print is large enough for easy reading, the sections are clearly distinguishable. Also, the front page is the only page which sends readers to other pages to complete the story. All other pages finish their stories on the page where they originate.

USA Today illustrates that superior writing focuses on people acting, thinking, and feeling. When this publication reports a national event, the reporter goes well beyond statistics or description of events. We see through the eyes of participants and witnesses.

Often you'll read offbeat stories here. The average home-town newspaper features family reunions of course. *USA Today* would describe a reunion by introducing us to stories behind the story—the relative who appears for the first time in thirty years, the inventor still seeking a patent after several hundred tries, the lifelong bachelor who brings a date nobody knows.

Another recommendation is *Reader's Digest.* For decades, the *Digest* has presented homespun humor, biographical sketches, and accounts of people overcoming huge obstacles, in an easily readable format.

For another top-ranking magazine, go to *People's Weekly,* known simply as *People.* No five-syllable words here, either. Just a breezy, bright, sometimes sarcastic look at celebrities, unknowns with high-interest potential, political figures, and athletes. The annual issue listing the "most beautiful people" sells out quickly.

I commend the editorial staffs of *Money, Kiplinger's,* and *Consumer's Digest* for presenting complex economic topics in readable language.

I'm sure you rely on helpful models I haven't mentioned. We can be grateful for those who write to communicate, not to impress.

TITLES

DO YOU WRITE AN ARTICLE, THEN FIND A TITLE? OR do you find the title first, then develop content consistent with the name you've selected?

Whichever method you use (and mine is to latch onto the title before I type the first word), choosing the right title sounds easy only to those who haven't tried it.

Years ago, I began sending freelance articles to news-papers. Only then did I learn—through my articles in print—that editors feel no obligation to use the author's title. Nor do they feel compelled to check with the author.

However, freelance writers need not think they're singled out, because the stories prepared by newspaper staff people *get their titles from other staff people.*

Book titles come from many directions. Norman Mailer didn't originate the name for his blockbuster novel, *The Naked and the Dead*. One evening he was talking about his manuscript to friends in a bar. A stranger who overheard the discussion suggested the eventual title. Mailer, according to bystanders, gave the stranger twenty-five dollars for his creativity, and passed the title on to his editor.

The title of the book you're reading matured through several weeks of deliberation among the publisher's staff.

Avid readers would be fascinated if they could see the authors' proposed titles for famous books. In some instances, the publisher's eventual selection bore no resemblance to the author's recommendation.

For the ultimate lesson in how titles affect sales, browse *National Enquirer*, *Globe*, and similar tabloids near the grocery checkout line. They *do* arrest your attention!

I consider these characteristics as *musts* for a good title:

Accurate. You can't promise more than you'll deliver. The title mirrors the content, without distortion.

Fair. A charitable organization sent the local paper a press release, announcing the kickoff of a major gifts campaign. The article stated proudly that 45 percent of the goal was raised in cash and pledges—a range fund-raisers find accept-able at launching time. However, the headline read *"Hospital raises 45% of campaign goal."* Readers who stopped with the title must have thought the campaign failed by missing the goal so drastically.

Concise. To learn how not to title your writing, read the titles of theses and dissertations published last year. In some cases, you'd think the title matched the treatise in length. Settle for a one word or two word title if you're fortunate enough to devise one. (Note: the one word heading for this entry says enough.)

Vivid. Among modern speeches, I know no better title than Dr. Martin Luther King Jr.'s *I Have a Dream.* Everyone dreams, everyone has fantasies. King selected a title his listeners *saw* as well as heard.

Memorable. Aren't all vivid titles memorable? No, but the best ones are. As with Dr. King's speech, those who recall the title move easily to recalling the speech.

Imaginative. I like for titles of articles, books, plays, poetry, speeches—any creation—to show a flair for fanciful thinking. *A Funny Thing Happened on the Way to the Forum* comes to mind. James Kilpatrick's book about writing carried the title *Fine Print.* Dr. Richard Carlson's *Don't Sweat the Small Stuff* uses a common expression to snag the browser. One of the most famous sermons on the revival circuit was *Payday Someday.*

What's in a name? Plenty. Write it right.

EDITING YOUR WRITING

WHEN YOU'RE WRITING FOR PUBLICATION, YOU know an editor will review your work. More likely, several editors may see your manuscript. They'll seek a consensus on whether to publish and what changes to recommend.

In our worst predictions, we anticipate editors running out of red ink as they mark passages they consider confusing, contradictory, dull, inaccurate, plagiaristic, verbose—and more. We wonder how they'll react to our punctuation, organization, title, and illustrations.

To reduce your fear of editors, *edit your writing so thoroughly yourself that other editors will have very little left to do or suggest.*

Admittedly, editing your work demands discipline. Writers share a common characteristic—the *Mail It Now!* syndrome. Once we get our thoughts on paper, we feel *driven* to share our masterpieces with a world that has been deprived of our enlightenment for too long. Alas, we don't want to keep people waiting another day. Almost as soon as we punch "save" on our keyboard, we look around for an envelope and postage.

The discipline becomes worthwhile when you know you are sending an editor your best effort.

What do you look for when you edit (assuming you have followed the steps for proofreading I've included in the section on letters)?

Start by gaining the fresh perspective that comes with tomorrow. Never complete your writing and start your extended editing the same day. Admittedly, you'll edit some as you write, and a bit more when you conclude a manuscript. However, for really serious analysis and revision, hold yourself in check until a new dawn.

One of my professors used the phrase *the clear light of another day.* I learned the wisdom of his advice. The next day the manuscript impresses us differently. Suddenly, the cute remark we wrote strikes us as an inept attempt at humor, an effort most readers will miss. We discover that we omitted an important part of an event we described. The conclusion seems weak. Just twenty-four hours after we gazed at our *magnum opus*, flaws come to the surface. They're real, unmistakable.

Why didn't we see them yesterday? We were too close to the action. Impossible to have much objectivity then. Now we'll read the article with slightly less pride of authorship.

In critiquing your writing, search for a number of writing faults, including these:

Too wordy. Enjoying words as much as we do, writers tend to overuse them. We'll take a page to say what could be said in a paragraph, a paragraph to say what we could have presented in a sentence. Okay if we're paid by the word, but we're not. Publications pay us according to *valuable thoughts we express concisely.*

Cut, yet retain the same meaning. "At this point in time" becomes "now."

62

Good writers keep the "delete" key busy. I've said enough on this. You understand. On to the next point.

Too monotonous in style. Every sentence has the same structure. Every noun has its verb. Every sentence has the same length. Every reader goes to sleep. Yes, they will! Catch yourself in a rut? Make the necessary changes.

Not enough people interacting. Thumb through any best-selling novel. As you speed through the pages, what jumps out at you? Quote marks. People are talking, exchanging ideas, confronting each other, inquiring. Gary Provost, in *Make Every Word Count*, affirms: "Putting flesh-and-bones people into your articles gives those articles a life and a movement that sets them apart from articles in which no one's heart is beating."

Provost and other leading writing teachers have observed that the strong distinctions between writing fiction and nonfiction have almost disappeared—so we can use (and are expected to use) the same stylistic boosters used by novelists, although we're writing for the company newsletter or a trade journal.

Too stilted. Mark through "pursuant to our most recent dialogue in your business establishment." Substitute "following up on our conversation in your office." Stuffy words conjure up visions of stuffed shirts. Try reading your manuscript aloud. Are you *sounding* like one person talking with another? If not, try again.

Adjective overload. Novice writers annoy readers by wearing out words such as marvelous, exquisite, fantastic, great, super, unbelievable, incredible. One dessert with a meal brings variety and a welcomed flavor change. Yet sitting down to a meal offering several desserts ushers in feelings of nausea. Remember how you react when you hear about pie-eating contests?

Passive voice instead of active. Passive shows a person receiving action: "The course was taken by Margaret." Active shows the person in charge: "Margaret took the course."

Trite expressions. Get rid of "fit as a fiddle," "in my humble opinion," "a sight for sore eyes" and similar expressions which have become meaningless through overuse. Search for creative ways to express yourself—*your* way, not the slang from twenty years ago.

Our checklist of what to look for in your editing could expand for pages. By now, though, you get an indication of how the writer becomes his or her own editor.

Grab your latest composition. Jot down the no-nos you want to eliminate. Now: *ready. . .set . . . edit!*

REVIEW YOUR WAY INTO PRINT

BEGINNING WRITERS COME UP EMPTY WHEN A newspaper editor says, "So, you want to write. Let me see some of your clips." In the journalism arena, *clips* stands for *clippings*—copies of articles we've published elsewhere.

The novice becomes puzzled. How do you get the clips without the first article, which itself seems to require clips?

Many writers who become occasional and even regular columnists with newspapers got the required clips by starting as reviewers.

For three years, I wrote book reviews for a metropolitan newspaper. Sure, there's competition by other writers who want to join the reviewing staff. However, if my experience is typical, you'll move ahead of other aspirants by following my example.

Call the book review editor and request an appointment. Tell the editor, "I read your section regularly. I believe I can write reviews that match the style and length you use. Also, I have several topics I can cover, depending upon your needs. What day and time next week are good for you?"

During your get-acquainted visit, hand the editor a page that includes:

Name, address, phone number, social security number

Educational background

Profession

Titles of ten major books you have read within the last three years

A short sample of your writing

Topics you're interested in

What qualifies you to review books in those areas

The editor will welcome your preparation. Give the editor a minute to read your page, then ask, "Do you need any additional information?"

Most likely, the answer will be no. Ask, "Would you like to assign some books to me now for reviews?"

This comment moves the conversation to the active phase. If the editor gives you two or three books, request deadline dates, plus written guidelines for reviewers. Mention how often you'll be able to write reviews—monthly, twice monthly, quarterly, whatever your preference.

Meet your deadlines, write intelligent, candid, interesting reviews, compare each author to others you have read, select provocative quotations . . . and you'll keep on getting assignments.

Your pay? Probably no dollars, but you'll acquire visibility and experience in evaluating and summarizing lengthy works using only a few paragraphs. You'll hone your writing skills, and benefit from regular interaction with the editor. And—you'll receive a steady flow of current books, on a complimentary basis.

As we said earlier, you'll accumulate clips. Collect copies, and you may find they're helpful in landing assignments for other departments with the same newspaper.

Well, what if your area doesn't publish a large newspaper? Test city and county newspapers in your locale. Since your reviewing service will cost them nothing, they may express interest. With smaller publications, you won't seek a full-time book editor to meet with. The front desk can guide you to the appropriate staff member.

Not interested in book reviews? How about reviewing plays, movies, and other cultural events? Here, too, small newspapers can benefit from your service. Use the same procedures suggested for book reviewers.

Writing about other writers paves the way for the day when other writers will review *you*.

GETTING PUBLISHED

I RANK GARY PROVOST VERY HIGH AMONG WRITING instructors. Not having had the privilege of attending his workshops, I know him through his books about writing. He practices what he preaches—writing that's clear, interesting, and informative.

In addition to his skills as a writing teacher, I profit every time I read about his long struggle to break into print. In his twenties, he wrote seven novels. He envisioned seeing them on bestseller lists. To his amazement, no publisher agreed. Provost "collected enough rejection slips to wallpaper a medium-sized garage."

Doggedly, he persisted. He overcame his anger long enough to admit his writing wasn't good enough for publication. He labored like any craftsman learning a trade. Ten years later, he had sold a romance novel, four novels for children, one book about writing, one sports book, two true-crime dramas, and two movies—along with hundreds of newspaper and magazine columns.

Provost doesn't recount his accomplishments to brag, but to show that there was a time of waiting and hoping for him, as for the majority of successful writers.

Change Your Communication—Change Your Life!

Probably his story appeals because I experienced the same tedious and tiring process. For a decade, I was *sure* I deserved to have my work published. Many hours over typewriters, many mailings . . . and many letters with the standard denial sentences: "Your material is not quite right for us at this time. We appreciate your submission. We are returning your manuscript, and trust you will find a publisher elsewhere." (Have a familiar ring?)

Eventually, I submitted an article I believed in more than any other I'd written. "Twentieth Anniversary Thoughts"described how college life had changed since I graduated. I sent copies, with cover letters, to fourteen editors.

All my life I'll remember the day the mail brought letters from two magazine editors, representing *College Today* and *College Board Review*. Each editor agreed to publish the manuscript. To my delight, each included a check for $100. In the mid 1970s, a check for that amount was noteworthy for novice writers.

Myriads of well-known authors could relate similar delays and disappointments. Getting into print demands (not just requires, *demands)* long-suffering patience and persistence. Writers lacking those traits fall by the wayside, saying, "It wasn't meant to be." Writers with those traits endure editors who tell them they have no writing talent, agents who decline to represent them, readers who call them boring.

Once you're armed with the never-quit attitude, observe these specific qualifications for pleasing editors:

Master your language. Be correct, be exciting in your writing.

Read widely. Steer away from imitating authors who excel, but see why they excel.

Start small. Send articles to your local paper before you try the *New York Times*.

Seek critiques. Find a writers group and attend workshops.

Subscribe to *Writer's Digest* or *The Writer.*

Explore the variety of publication opportunities—company reports, greeting cards, trade magazines, and others.

Find your niche. You can't claim expertise on everything. Stick with your qualifications.

Submit manuscripts as near to being perfect as possible. Typos and misspellings damage credibility.

Read samples of the publications you have targeted. Determine what they want.

Request writer's guidelines, and follow them unfailingly.

Query editors. Sell yourself and your idea.

Keep expectations realistic.

Think of writing as *work*. To reap joy, you'll have to sow silent, lonely, exhausting hours of researching, writing, editing, rewriting.

Remain passionate about your message. I assume you have one. Otherwise, why write?

The day your byline accompanies an article or your name adorns a book jacket, you'll know—as only other writers know—that your patience, persistence, and adherence to the basic requirements were gloriously worthwhile.

HOW ABOUT THOSE HOW-TO AUTHORS?

IN THIS SECTION ABOUT WRITING, YOU COULD EASILY think of the authors who produce advice books. There are so many of them. *Books in Print* lists more than five thousand books whose titles begin with *How to*. Sometimes statistics appear hard to believe, but not that one. Every bookstore displays an abundance of books in which experts (self-appointed or otherwise) give instructions for altering our attitudes and habits.

A number of these books have helped me. For example, twenty years ago I bought Alan Lakein's *How to Get Control of Your Time and Your Life.* Lakein's simply written volume enabled me to start making maximum use of my hours and days.

And I remember a book about speed reading that helped me get through the massive assignments I faced in graduate school.

Maybe you have your favorite how-to books. (In fact, I hope the book you're reading will become one of them!)

Let's admit, though, that not all how-to books are helpful. As with any category of books, some accomplish what they promise, others don't. As you face the dozens of books in the self-help section, how do you decide which ones to buy?

First, look at the author's claims. You'll believe a weight-loss authority if the book jacket promises moderate weight loss. However, if the book's description guarantees you'll lose thirty pounds a month, put the book back on the shelf.

Next, check the author's credentials. If the writer describes a super method for increasing your sales productivity, ask if he or she has ever sold anything—other than seminars, tapes, and books about selling. To illustrate: I'm inclined to buy books and tapes by Zig Ziglar, because I'm familiar with his background. Before he became a superstar speaker and trainer, he excelled in selling various products, including cookware.

On this point, note whether the book jacket includes testimonials from authorities in this field. I can assure you, nationally recognized authorities don't write endorsements for everyone who wants them. They know they're putting their reputations on the line. So a strong endorsement from an expert carries credibility.

Then skim the book to look at the author's supporting material. Does the author cite sources other than himself? If not, why not? Unfamiliar with other writers on the topic? Not willing to mention the competition?

Finally, include this important step: *find detailed practical procedures the author provides for readers*. After all, that's what *how-to* implies by definition. Self-help books must offer help—help you identify easily and put into action immediately.

GHOST WRITERS

THE TERM "GHOST WRITERS" EMERGES MOST frequently, I think, when we talk about those who assist American presidents with speeches, press releases, position papers, and opening statements for press conferences. "Ghost" implies they are around somewhere, inconspicuously preparing material—though not very visible during the delivery of a speech or publication of a book.

Ted Sorensen worked so closely with President Kennedy that Sorensen commented, "When Kennedy is cut, I bleed." His remark reflects the ghost's chief assignment—to embody the speaker's style so closely that even scholars have difficulty detecting what the speaker composed or edited and where the ghost came in.

Peggy Noonan, Roger Ailes—we can add plenty of names to the list of political ghosts.

Certainly ghosts circulate beyond politics. In corporate life, CEOs call on staff or freelancers to draft—or write in entirety—letters, mission statements, the executive's page in magazines and annual reports, along with various other pieces. Perhaps this explains why CEOs express reluctance to fire a top public relations team member. Wordsmiths aren't so easy to replace, particularly those who shape the executive's language so skillfully.

The book world is ghost-ridden, with those ghosts who remain anonymous and those who gain acclaim because of their associations. In the latter case, the author admits the writing was not done alone. So the book jacket lists the ghost, crediting him or her as the scribe. A movie star's book is "as told to Claude Rankin" or "with Claude Rankin." The reader remains puzzled about the celebrity's degree of participation in the writing.

What's the ethical judgment about ghosts? The debate has gone on for decades.

Purists contend that executives practice deceit by paying others to make the executive appear more informed and articulate than the executive would without scriptwriters.

Realists say the executive cannot possibly direct a large corporation if stockholders expect him to research every topic, write every speech, compose every letter, pen every memorandum.

Almost thirty years ago, I wrote about this topic for the first time. I wasn't blazing scholarly trails. Rhetorical historians point to early ghostwriters like Lysias, who prepared speeches for those wanting to excel in the courtrooms of ancient Athens, where citizens defended themselves. Lysias and his compatriots were called *logographers*. Occasionally, they researched legal aspects of cases to strengthen their speeches.

At any rate, my stance as a young speech-communication student was unyielding. I granted no tolerance for anyone at any level who sought help in writing hard copy or speeches. At the time, I wouldn't have predicted that, as an administrator, I would become the composer for several college presidents.

Did those experiences mellow my initial obdurance? Some, I'll grant. I learned that the reclusive, scholarly life required for superlative writing can hardly fit in a week which exceeds sixty hours anyway, dealing with what I often label *administrivia*.

Yet I draw the line on one point. No executive, alleged author, statesman, or columnist should ever claim 100 percent authorship if that's not the case.

I'm acquainted with authors who publish books written by people they have paid to write—but conceal the collaboration. Candidly, I consider them dishonest. I have no argument with writers who add "as told to" or "with." But those who assert, "I wrote this book" when they didn't, lose credibility with me.

I read a good analogy, likening the author who says "I did it all" to the person who hangs a painting another created, yet places only his own signature in the lower right corner. No way I can call the act legitimate.

So, must the CEO give credit to his marketing and public relations staff for sculpting a major pronouncement? Personally, I'd have greater respect for the executive who announces, "What I'm saying speaks for my team, whose words and thoughts helped design my statement."

Ghosts, you see, don't frighten me as much when I can see them.

WRITE IT OR SAY IT?

FOUR FACTORS HELP US DECIDE WHETHER TO send a message in writing or speak the message, either to an individual or group.

One is *the likely emotional impact of the message.* Today's lunch menu for the cafeteria, the housekeeping schedule for next week, and the announcement of a July the Fourth holiday seem safe enough to send by e-mail, bulletin board, or newsletter. In such cases, the words literally "speak for themselves"—clearly, simply, with almost no chance of causing hostility.

Other types of messages call for the calming influence of a person who is, as they say on television, "live on the scene." I have in mind statements like these:

> *"This time next year we'll have a work force that's reduced by 25 percent."*

> *"This quarter's production was disappointing, and we need to find the causes."*

> *"The books didn't balance this month. We've scheduled an audit of the accounting department."*

Threatening news becomes immeasurably more dire when we read the words without hearing details, and without the opportunity to ask questions and offer opinions.

Second is *the degree of permanence desired.* Spoken words disappear quickly. Too, what little we do remember suffers from distortion. Once in awhile, we'll record an important meeting through audio or video. More frequently, though, conversations and group deliberations are not retrievable.

Permanence requires writing. Memos, minutes, letters, "white papers," job descriptions—they come to our rescue when participants in dialogue stray from original agreements. There's some validity to the claim we're becoming a "paperless society." But we're going to write *on something,* in the interest of keeping records and delineating responsibilities.

A third factor is the *degree of formality intended.* You allow the speaker greater latitude in language. When a well-educated speaker declares, "That just *ain't gonna happen,"* you know the speaker has used the incorrect form to add emphasis.

Writing, except in the case of humorists, requires conformity to accepted standards.

Fourth, *whether you want instantaneous feedback* guides your choice. The writer may get delayed feedback—or none. The speaker hears comments and watches nonverbal reactions *while the message is in process.* Speakers enjoy the privilege of adjusting content and delivery to improve understanding and degree of persuasion.

A final note: The communicator confronts situations where the choice becomes *both,* rather than *either/or.* For example, in a company's crisis, you arrange a press conference, where you speak and distribute a news release. Next, you answer questions. Written and oral presentations combined strengthen your case well beyond what either method could accomplish alone.

WHEN YOUR FAVORITE WRITER WRITES NO MORE

HIS BOOK COVERS CAUGHT MY EYE FOR YEARS before I browsed the contents. Eventually, curiosity caused me to thumb through *The Return of the Ragpicker.*

Right away, I knew the author was an accomplished story-teller. Although he avoided the common ingredients of violence, lust, and profanity, he wrote "page-turners." He quipped that the only four-letter word in his books is *love*.

So I bought the book, and read the story quickly. The main character, Simon Potter, the "Ragpicker," became my friend and role model. That's why I purchased *The Greatest Miracle in the World*, where Simon originated.

Next, I turned to *The Greatest Salesman in the World*. The "hype type" on the back cover mentioned more than two million copies in print. I found out why. The author spun an intriguing saga about a first-century boy named Hafid, who left a caravan to seek wealth through a sales career—and discovered secrets of success for all who market their goods and services.

Next came *The Twelfth Angel*, with a contemporary setting, featuring Timothy, a frail boy who dreamed of playing on a baseball team. He wasn't blessed with athletic ability. Yet his buoyant spirit excited his teammates.

Like all authors, my favorite one penned an occasional dud. *The Choice* emerged as a poor parody of his earlier publications. *The Spellbinder's Gift* struck me the same way.

Now, back to the good ones. On vacation, I read *A Better Way to Live*, a compelling summary of the author's philosophy. With stark candor, he told how his first marriage and career failed, how he wandered the country with only a bottle for his friend, considered suicide—then, adapting a new approach, turned his life in a winning direction.

Being such a devoted admirer, I suffered a jolt when I read an advertisement for his works, including the notation: 1923–1996. That's how I learned he had died. Amazing—publishers sold thirty-six million copies of his books, he spoke at hundreds of conferences, recorded bestselling audiotapes, but died without widespread notice.

My favorite writer, Og Mandino, will write no more. I'll miss the excitement of opening a new book from him every year or two. But whenever I want, I'll visit him again, merely by turning the pages bearing his handiwork.

Great writers leave us, yes. Fortunately, their warm and wise thoughts last forever. My shelves overflow with these bound treasures. I trust yours do, too.

4

LETTER WRITING

THE MAN STOOD AT THE COUNTER, TALKING WITH the managers of the secretarial-services business. "Thanks for getting these letters ready," he said. "Now I'll just send them to prospective employers after I write the names and addresses and my hellos to the people on the list."

An awkward silence followed. The owner tried to be tactful. "Sir, I advise you not to do that."

"Why? I don't have a typewriter. And my handwriting is okay."

"Yes, sir, I'm sure it is. But unless you have the headings and salutations typed, all of these letters will go into the wastebasket without being read."

"Hey, you've seen my résumé," he continued, a bit disturbed. "My credentials are excellent. Isn't that what employers want?"

"That's really important, as you say. Yet they'll see this letter on top of your résumé. The quality of your letter tells them whether to read further."

With a defeated tone, the customer handed the letters back across the counter. "Guess you know more than I do about this. Type them for me. Will they be ready Thursday?"

As a history major, I learned that letters written by many famous people furnished special insight into their lives. Judging by the above illustration, we still use letters as yardsticks of the writer's tact, language skills, protocol, likability, professional potential, and a host of other attributes.

What about reading this chapter before your next trip to the post office?

TREASURED LETTERS

THE HOSPITAL VOLUNTEER SAID, "I'M NOT AS BUSY here as I used to be. My assignment is to deliver mail to patients. Years ago, that kept me busy. Now, though, people don't write as many personal letters."

Her comments disturbed me. I started thinking about how meaningful letters are at various stages of our lives.

The child at camp, struggling with homesickness, receives a letter from home. Reading the letter prompts memories: the smell of a home-cooked meal, sounds of loving voices, a mental picture of the child's bedroom, and hugs from caring parents. Whatever the content, the letter communicates, "You're loved, you're missed, we're thinking about you, and hoping you're having a great summer."

The college student welcomes letters, too. They ease the burden of exams, career decisions, boring assignments, roommate problems.

For many of us, letters have kindled romance. In my case, I married "the girl next door." We started dating in our teens, then went separate ways for awhile. During my graduate school days, I wrote her a letter, suggesting another try. Much later, she told me, "When I got your letter out of my mailbox, I put aside the letter I was about to mail to you. Mine said essentially what yours did." Ah, and what if neither of us had written. . . .

Not surprisingly, a few years ago we both enjoyed a movie which showed the consequences in the lives of three people when letters to them went undelivered. Misunderstandings, broken relationships, and sadness followed.

Biographers, of course, rely heavily on letters between famous couples. Topping the list would be those between Robert Browning and Elizabeth Barrett Browning. In more modern times, letters from H. L. Mencken to his wife appeared in book form.

Letters make milestones in our lives more heartwarming and memorable. I imagine you have a collection of letters with statements like these:

"Congratulations on your promotion. I know you'll do a good job, as you always do."

"We enjoyed visiting your new home. May you have many happy years there."

"We share your loss. Your father was one of our favorite people, as you know. The funeral service gave wonderful tribute to him and his achievements."

"Your new career sounds exciting. Keep us posted on your progress."

"So, you have retired at last. Hopefully, this will give you time to come our way more often. Have fun with your new-found freedom!"

Letters allow us to express admiration to those we admire. Some respond, others don't. In my experience, several of my heroes have written back—Dr. Benjamin Spock, Coretta Scott King, and golfer Ken Venturi are among them.

For these reasons and more, I encourage all of us to get away from computer correspondence long enough to compose a "hard copy" letter to friends, family, new acquaintances, long absent colleagues, and strangers who need our good words.

Wouldn't it be nice if your mailbox contained hand-addressed letters that *are not* engagement and graduation announcements, or invitations to parties? Send personalized letters, and you'll begin to get some of those treasured letters yourself.

"AS WE DISCUSSED . . ."

YOU'VE HAD THE APPOINTMENT. THE CONVERSATION seemed to go well. From your observations, you and the other person reached agreement on major issues. Additionally, you agreed on what should happen next.

"But wait," you caution yourself, "I've felt the same way before—confident, assured of a sale, partnership, merger, or other business transaction. To my surprise, I learned a few weeks later how wrong I had been. And I promised myself that next time I'd follow up with a letter about the meeting. *This* is the time to carry through on my self-commitment."

How can you do so tactfully? Amazingly, three words will perform magic. The words—to be used when you begin to recap the meeting—are "As we discussed."

This opener works because you're declaring a *team effort*. You're not speaking for yourself alone. *We* includes rather than excludes. Contrast this approach with "As I said." Much different, don't you think?

The word "discussed" has positive psychological impact, too. Discussion implies free-flowing exchange of ideas, openness, listening. In my experience, "discussion" accomplishes even more than "agreed." It's less threatening, less final. "Yeah," the other party will say, "she's right. We did discuss that item."

Using this introductory phrase, you'll reiterate major points considered, problems identified, responsibilities of each person in addressing problems, and details such as budget, deadlines, what's public information and what is not, personnel implications—the entire range of topics covered.

To close your letter, do you ask for feedback about your version? There's no standard answer. In cases involving legal matters, you're likely to request written confirmation.

In more general instances, leave the way open—again, with a low key invitation: "Please let me know if you have anything to add to my summary." Notice we didn't say "to correct." "Correct" waves a red flag, suggesting mistakes. "Add to" says nothing negative about your version.

Employed tactfully, "As we discussed" will prevent misunderstandings, encourage teamwork, and generate a written record which will be valuable in preparing for future meetings.

Complaint Letters

MANY OF US PERFORM A VERY IMPORTANT ACTIVITY— writing complaint letters. It's important because we experience dissatisfaction we want to express. Also, in some instances we have a monetary loss to recover.

As voice mail has become more popular, unhappy clients can't reach the persons they need to talk with, fostering an increase in the use of letters to state grievances.

An effective complaint letter opens with the right tone. While the word "complaint" implies we're unhappy, we must put a checkrein on our emotions when we start writing. Why? Because a letter filled with accusations, nasty words, and threats won't generate positive responses.

I recommend starting your letter with a statement like "I have a problem I need to call to your attention," or even "With your reputation for good service, I'm sure you'll want to know about an unfortunate incident."

Speaking of *incident* moves us to the next point. Make your complaint specific. Rather than saying, "One of your sales clerks was rude," mention the salesperson's name, the date and time, the exact words you remember, and similar details. A manager might ignore generalities, but will evaluate an itemized complaint.

Another strategy is to say what you believe the company must do to resolve the grievance. Your suggestion indicates you have thought constructively. "I want an apology," "I request a refund," or "I want the merchandise replaced" provide possible solutions.

Also, state your willingness to talk about the problem. List your phone numbers. With a local business, request an appointment. List three dates/times you're available for an appointment.

When you're dealing with highly sensitive matters, mainly those where legal issues emerge, send copies to appropriate officials. Below your signature, note who will receive copies. Refer to the recipients in your letter if you choose.

I've written my share of complaint letters, and I can assure you these steps bring results.

ANSWERING COMPLAINT LETTERS

BEGIN WITH THIS ASSUMPTION: EVERY COMPLAINT letter merits an answer, as long as the writer supplies a signature and an address. Yes, this holds true even with letters reflecting uncontrolled temper, sarcasm, personal attacks, inappropriate language, threats of taking business elsewhere, claims of influence with company executives—name the problem, the letter still calls for a reply.

Consider that one reason for the letter is the customer's feeling of being ignored. To ignore the customer by silence fans the animosity.

Assume, too, the complaint letter deserves a prompt answer—prompt as within a week of receipt. The letter may question the company's efficiency. We don't want to support the writer's argument by delay.

Our reply has to be personal. About ten years ago, I wrote a letter to the president of a major university expressing my unhappiness because he decided two academically ineligible students should play in the upcoming football bowl game. When his reply came, I was sure the letter I received was a replica of one sent to every other complaining author. A few months afterward, one of the president's staff people told me, "Oh, yes. Everybody got the same letter. How do I know? Because I wrote the letter for the president's signature."

Since the complaint letter originated from an individual, receivers must give the reply a personalized touch. Any letter smacking of "to whom it may concern" dips in credibility the instant the reader opens the page.

Which brings me to the next point. The reply ought to address *every specific complaint* the customer made. The university president's letter to me floundered about in generalities. I had made at least a half dozen observations worthy of his comments. Among them: I was a former faculty member there, my wife had worked at the university, both daughters graduated there. The president acknowledged none of these connections.

Obviously, taking a defensive position—"You're mistaken, we're not"—creates more hostility. The complainer reacts by feeling accused of lying. Questioning a writer's accuracy, and with even poorer judgment lambasting his motives, alienates. The wise manager apologizes for inconvenience, poor quality, rudeness—whatever the perceived mistreatment.

For the next step, the manager offers reasonable compensation and courtesy: "Please accept the enclosed gift certificate." "We are crediting your account with the refund." "I invite you to come to my office the next time you visit our store."

The letter signifies who is getting a copy. The reader thinks, "Good, the manager is contacting those who were involved directly."

On the day you send the letter, mark your calendar (which may exist as computer software) or tickler file to follow up with a letter or call two to three weeks later. Following up reflects your *continuing concern.*

Continuing concern, I'm sure you know, results in continuing customers.

CAN YOU PROOF IT?

YOU'VE HAD THIS EXPERIENCE, I IMAGINE. YOU MAIL an important letter—applying for a job or presenting a sales proposal. You labored diligently to say the right thing. You're proud of the letter. Then the next day, as you're filing the item, you come across a "typo." Your stomach turns. How could this happen? You read the letter several times. Now you wish you could recall the faulty copy, but you can't.

There's no reason to feel paranoid about the error. Typos are incredibly common.

The editor of a small town newspaper grew weary of the published errors readers kept mentioning to him. So he announced in an editorial that the following Thursday would feature an "error-free" edition. He offered an unusual reward to eagle-eyed readers, vowing to deliver a twenty-five-cent piece to the first person to call him about every misprint.

To his surprise, he stayed very busy that Thursday, delivering quarters to the first spotters of thirty-seven misprints.

You can guess he never repeated the offer.

When I teach workshops for secretaries, administrative assistants, and receptionists, I distribute copies of typos I have collected. And invariably, workshop participants share their experience with hapless misspellings and misplaced letters.

I recall the write-up of a college football game. A photo caption claimed the quarterback had passed for 243 "years." Though the game must have seemed very long to the losing team, the word should have been "yards."

My college's alumni magazine printed a testimonial from a prominent graduate. According to the publication, he declared he could not "underestimate" the value of a Millsaps College education. Clearly, "overestimate" was the intended word.

Another typo carried comic results. A college's newsletter, in attempting to boost attendance at a basketball game, promised a "fowl" shooting contest at halftime. Alas, "foul" got fouled up.

Letter writers cannot turn to spell check with complete confidence. The example above illustrates the problem. *Fowl* is spelled correctly, so spell check won't flag the word for correction. Spell check helps, of course, but we need additional devices. I offer the following, which others recommend, too:

Read the printed text backward. This way, you won't become lost in meaning. You're more apt to examine individual words.

Isolate a line at a time. Place a ruler under the line, or an envelope—anything to block out the print below. I've heard of clerical assistants who cut holes in cardboard, leaving an opening about the size of a typed line.

Circulate the letter among your colleagues. One reader may find what another misses.

Ask someone who is unfamiliar with the material to proof the letter. They won't be misled by the expectations that color your reading.

Put the letter aside until the next day. One of my graduate professors taught, "The clear light of another day increases your objectivity."

Read the letter aloud. Possibly you'll catch grammatical mistakes overlooked in silent reading.

By the way, if you use proofing tips I haven't mentioned, I'll be happy to hear about them.

Well, what if you use every method you know, and the ones I advocate, and typos creep into your letters anyway? Just remember your readers will be tolerant. They've made a fair share of bloopers themselves.

THE ENVELOPE, PLEASE

THE FUND-RAISING OFFICE OF A MAJOR UNIVERSITY followed a fairly standard practice. When a staff member visited a prospective contributor, he or she wrote two items shortly afterward. One was a thank-you letter, expressing appreciation for the prospect's time and interest in the institution. Depending upon how the visit went, the writer might encourage the alumnus or friend to consider a contribution during the current year. Usually, the writer requested a designation for a specific fund.

The development officer's other item was a "call report" for office use summarizing the visit. Staff members write these quickly. To ensure accuracy, they may record them in a portable dictaphone before they return to campus. A typical call report might include the prospect's family news, business accomplishments, and attitudes toward the university, in addition to problems needing the university president's attention, and appropriate next steps.

On the day I visited this university's office, the team looked downcast. Before long, I learned why. The previous week, a staff member had visited one of the university's greatest potential benefactors. The follow-up proceeded as planned—

letter of appreciation and call report.

Needing an outsider to express their turmoil to, their vice president informed me: "Bill, pardon us for not showing the hospitality level you expected. It's nothing personal against you. We're in a horrible frame of mind, and I'll tell you why."

John showed me a letter from the prospect, received that morning. The letter let John know about a disastrous mix-up. An employee had mailed the call report *to the prospect*. What went into the prospect's file? Why, the gracious thank-you letter!

In a brief, but unmistakably forthright letter, the prospect said the university's description of him was flawless. They were right to categorize him as a "crusty, tight old SOB, who'll never give us a dime."

My stomach tightened as I read the farewell letter—which indeed it was. I wondered whether the employee had been talking to a passerby, rushing for a lunch outing, working from a clutter-filled desk, or was beset with a family problem that day.

Whatever the reason, the university lost a major gift, the good reputation of the office (I assume the prospect shared his chagrin with his friends), tranquility—and, I imagine, a clerical support person.

Have you ever received a letter meant for someone else? Feels weird, I assure you, as the following story illustrates.

When I looked at the envelope from an educational institution, I couldn't guess why they were writing me. Picture my surprise when the letter used the traditional phrases for rejecting my job application. "Although you have excellent skills and experience, you were not chosen for an interview," I read. The closing line said the writer "will be happy to hold your résumé in our file for future openings."

Nice way to treat an applicant. Agreed? Trouble was, I had not applied there. However disorganized I might seem at times, at least I know where I send my credentials. As you'll suppose, I didn't bother to reply.

Whimsically, I jested that my career had dropped to a new low, now that I was getting rejected *prior to* my application.

Let's grant, though, that you're looking at a letter which came to the right place. What else could go wrong with the envelope? Well, at times you've probably seen disturbing variations on the spelling of your last name. Strangely, the letterhead spelled your name correctly. The linguistic massacre occurred only on the envelope.

And yes, I'm sure you've had to pay postage due on letters, because there was no stamp at all or one for less than the required amount.

Envelopes arrive with ink smudges, with smudges from candy and soft drinks, with cigarette burns, with enough wrinkles to make you wonder where the envelope box was stored. (Granted, some of this may be attributed to the postal service.)

"But," a professional person asks, "do CEOs see envelopes? Doesn't an assistant open the mail, discarding the envelopes to reduce disorder?"

Maybe, maybe not. There's no guarantee the assistant won't say, "Thought you'd want to see the botched-up envelope that brought this letter. Here it is. Says something about the sender, I think."

The upshot of these considerations: *envelopes communicate*, just as letters do. They talk about our efficiency, accuracy, neatness, and style. They communicate a professional image *before* the receiver gets to the letter.

Let's package our letters with care and pride.

5

GIVING SPEECHES

CICERO HELD A PREEMINENT POSITION AMONG early teachers of oratory. One of his simplest observations carries a ring of timelessness: "For it is by this one gift that we are most distinguished from brute animals, that we converse together, and can express our thoughts by speech."

Fortunately—in spite of widespread fears to the contrary— proficiency in speaking is not confined to an elite few. In my years of teaching, I've watched many aspiring speakers move from almost numb silence to fluent, confident speaking.

Years ago, I quit predicting who would captivate an audience and who wouldn't. One university student named Elaine comes to mind. Until her first speech, she sat silently, withdrawn from her classmates. I don't think I had heard her voice before she rose to give her first classroom speech. Almost miraculously, she became a different person. To my bewilderment, she entertained the class with stories about how she and others in a high-school gang had made counterfeit drivers' licenses. An unbelievable turnaround!

Elaine and so many other speakers have demonstrated that *every person who can articulate words can learn to address an audience.*

Disregard your previous precautions about speaking. Absorb this chapter's recommendations. Soon you'll welcome audiences with the same energy you once used to dodge them.

BE YOURSELF

THE WRITINGS OF RALPH WALDO EMERSON, OFTEN taken from his lectures, offer timeless advice on various topics. Among the passages I have underlined and circled: "Imitation is suicide." He explains, "I must be myself."

Related to communication, successful speakers accept who they are, including both assets and liabilities.

The early teachers of rhetoric—Quintilian, Aristotle, and Cicero—advised students to watch and learn from prominent orators, including their teachers. Role models illustrated the qualities of the orator. Still, they cautioned against excessive imitation. Cicero said the tendency was to imitate the worst qualities, since they were the easiest to duplicate. He said the truly gifted speakers relied on imitation very little.

I remember when evangelist Billy Graham gained national recognition. By the end of his career, Graham spoke to more people in live audiences than any other public figure. Add to that his vast television audience, and you have one of the world's most watched and most listened to speakers.

As Graham's popularity increased, so did his imitators. Preachers adopted broad, sweeping gestures, held the Bible high with one hand, increased their rate of speech, and displayed other Grahamisms. Predictably, most of them turned away listeners. There's *only one* Billy Graham. Impostors looked unnatural . . . because they were.

I imagine you have seen those who copied Dr. Martin Luther King Jr.'s language, sprinkling alliteration, metaphors, and parallel construction throughout their speeches. Those stylistic devices worked well with King. However, when we hear copycats, we think of King, not them. How can a speaker be satisfied in turning the audience's thoughts back several decades to another speaker?

Those who judged debate contests in the years just after the assassinations of John and Robert Kennedy confronted Kennedy replicas. Students assumed the Kennedy cockiness, gestured with index fingers pointing downward, and smiled or paused to signal the end of a point.

Sadly, some of those students didn't find out *who they were* as speakers.

With this in mind, I caution speakers against too much rehearsal. A moderate amount teaches us timing, raises confidence, and improves memory. Moving beyond the optimum level, we run the risk of *imitating ourselves*. This may be as harmful as imitating someone else.

I confess to attempting imitations earlier in my speaking career. They didn't work, I assure you. I can only be me, speaking to an individual or to a group.

To achieve this, let's keep Og Mandino's words nearby:

"I am a unique creature. . . . Since the beginning of time never has there been another with my mind, my heart. . . . I will capitalize on this difference for it is an asset to be promoted to the fullest. . . . I am rare, and there is value in all rarity."

WHAT ABOUT MY ACCENT?

YOU MAY HAVE SEEN ADVERTISEMENTS FOR ADULT education classes which promise, "You'll get rid of your accent within five weeks."

Because our accents form over a period of years, our first question would be, "Is this possible?"

The second spontaneous question: "Even if the class can accomplish elimination of accents, is this either necessary or desirable?"

Before we move toward an answer, let's note that regional accents aren't nearly as prominent as they were thirty years ago. Today's forty year olds grew up listening to a new invention, television. Except for local broadcasts, most spoken language on the tube cannot be pigeonholed into a region.

Change Your Communication—Change Your Life!

National newscasters, reporters, commentators, and analysts escape geographical identity. Listeners rarely say with certainty, "Oh, I know where *he's* from."

Mobility of the population has reduced conspicuous accents. No longer bound to a fifty-mile radius for life, families hear and imitate—consciously or accidentally—speech styles across the country.

I marvel at how suddenly we modify accents. Young couples who move to a new city, then welcome their parents for a visit a month later, hear their visitors say, "You're starting to talk like people around here. What's happened to you?"

No, accents aren't so obvious now. Still, they do persist. What, then, about these courses promising a "cure"?

I'll offer a simple answer. If you anticipate lifelong residence in your present locale, pay no attention to your accent. In your social and business contacts, you'll talk with people who *don't even know you have an accent*—primarily because you speak like them.

On the other hand, the professionally mobile person (which means traveling extensively and/or moving to contrasting regions) needs to consider whether speech habits pose a distraction.

Also, evaluate how an accent affects your job performance. As we hinted at the outset, the accent must go when a person plans a career in broadcasting, acting, or similar professions such as teaching or professional speaking and training before diverse audiences.

For those who decide to alter their accents, I vote against the five-week cram course, except as a starting point. Other choices include enrolling in speech courses (academic or noncredit), hiring a speech/voice coach, rehearsing with a tape recorder, and listening to tapes of speakers with general American dialect.

I offer these observations as a communication professional. Speaking personally, I grew up in Mississippi, and every visit there brings back those speech tones which emit a fragrance as captivating as the magnolias.

THE RIGHT STUFF FOR YOUR INTRODUCTION

WE ALL KNOW THE VALUE OF A SUPPORTIVE introduction. In a prestigious group, you experience a special glow when a respected colleague says, "I want you to meet a special friend of mine. He is one of the leaders in our field. I encourage you to talk with him for a few minutes during the reception. You'll find his ideas exceptionally worthwhile."

Contrast the effect of that endorsement with, "Here's somebody I brought along. Let me interrupt your important conversations for just a second to introduce him."

When we stand to face an audience, what has our introducer done to establish our credibility? In worst case scenarios, what harm has the host inflicted?

With forethought and preparation, the speaker has an opportunity to coach the host, so the host will stimulate expectations properly. Leaving such an important factor to chance runs too much risk.

Professional speakers (who earlier in their careers thought the host would perform admirably without instruction) could relate enough horror stories to fill this book. Samples:

"Idelle recommended him as our speaker. She hasn't heard him. I haven't either. Here he is—see what you think."

"We weren't going to have a speaker, but at the last minute a few of us decided we might need one. Without further ado, here she is."

Believe me, any effort that prevents those embarrassing and depressing introductions is well worthwhile.

Following is the plan professional speakers use.

Step one: Select the person who will introduce you. While this may not be possible in every case, a tactful inquiry may bring the person you want to the lectern—the top officer in the organization. Ordinarily, no one else has the clout the group's leader carries.

Step two: Talk with your introducer. Determine whether he will remain for the entire program. Why? Because the introducer's presence or absence triggers an opinion from the audience. A ceremonial introducer who remarks, "I wish I could stay to hear this fine presentation" reveals his priorities. We all want the introducer to include, "I have been looking forward to this occasion, just as you have. Our speaker has established a solid reputation in our industry. I'm glad to share your opportunity to hear him now."

What if the scheduled introducer admits he'll depart when you rise to speak? Graciously, explain why his exit will raise serious questions. Request a change in his schedule, or another person to present you.

Step three: Tell your introducer: "I'm so pleased you'll introduce me. Since you don't have time, with all your responsibilities, to read my bio sketch, I'm going to send you a brief introduction. Please use what I send—and call me if you have questions I need to answer." Most presenters will applaud your effort to save their time.

Step four: Write and send an introduction which establishes your credentials, demonstrating concisely why you're the right choice for the occasion. In capsuling your qualifications, err on the side of modesty. Audiences dislike lengthy rehashing of honors and achievements. Highlight only those with utmost relevance for the audience. Confine your copy to no more than three quarters of a page, double-spaced.

Step five: Make your follow-up call, rather than waiting for theirs: "Did you receive the introduction I mailed? Everything look all right?"

Step six: Bring an extra copy of the introduction to the event. Hosts misplace the copy you mailed, or forget where they filed it. A backup copy will increase your peace of mind as the hour arrives.

Step seven: As you and the introducer talk on the way into the meeting hall, thank the person again for hosting you.

Step eight: Have an appropriate remark ready, to thank this person in your first comments to the audience. If he included *the right stuff,* he deserves your applause and theirs.

STAGE FRIGHT NEED NOT BE FATAL

COMEDIAN JERRY SEINFELD READ A SURVEY THAT ranked the fear of public speaking higher than the fear of death. He commented, "Judging by that survey, if I go to a funeral I should feel more sympathy for the speaker than for the corpse."

To quote Roger Ailes, a former speech coach for presidents, "even heroes get scared" when they face an audience. I agree. When I taught speech communication at the University of Georgia, I saw varsity football players—who played with sixty thousand fans watching—lose their poise when giving a speech to twenty classmates.

I'll bet you know their symptoms: sweaty palms, dry throat, shaky knees, quivering lips, an unsteady voice, a stammering tongue, shortness of breath, and memory loss.

But notice . . . these reactions don't prove fatal. In reading obituaries, you'll never find "stage fright" listed as the cause of death.

How do speakers cope with stage fright successfully? How can you?

First, remember that the speaker notices the symptoms, but listeners don't. Who will feel your cold hands or know your pulse rate has increased? To prove this, videotape your speech. Watching the replay, you'll decide: "Say, people couldn't see my physical responses."

Second, place the speech situation in the appropriate framework. When Lincoln said, "The world will little note nor long remember what we say here," he was mistaken about himself—but correct about us.

Think about the speakers at your civic club last month. Who were they, and what did they say? You may not remember. Go back even another month—and you recall even less. The lesson: no need to get agitated over an event which fades so quickly.

Third, prepare thoroughly. Knowing your material increases confidence. Some speakers review their notes silently, some rehearse aloud, some do both. Find the method which saturates your mind with main ideas, key words, and lively illustrations. *Preparation* will reduce your *perspiration!*

Fourth, change your concept of audiences—from seeing them as critics to seeing them as cheerleaders. Most listeners *want you to succeed.* Silently, they're muttering, "I'm glad she's up there speaking, and not me. She's got a tough job, and I'm pulling for her."

Fifth, expect imperfection, and accept it. You're likely to say "uh." You'll mispronounce words, even forget a favorite quote. You'll leave out important points. However, the audience welcomes these signals that an ordinary person is sharing ideas. Listeners prefer hearing a few blunders to watching a robot deliver a flawless recitation.

Sixth, forget about making an impression. Focus on talking about beliefs that excite you. Ironically, you'll make your finest impression then. "You're a super speaker" sounds nice, but treasure this comment instead: "You really helped my thinking on that subject."

Seventh, welcome a moderate degree of fear as your friend. Just as athletes want to "get up for the game," you'll benefit from some anxiety. Channeled creatively, fear energizes us and our listeners.

Try these tips. They've worked for plenty of nervous presenters—including me.

CONSIDER EVERY AUDIENCE IMPORTANT

A FRIEND OF MINE, COLONEL GERALD GRAHAM, described a memorable incident involving Bob Hope during World War II. Bob and his well-known partner, Jerry Colonna, came to a New Guinea army base to entertain the troops. Colonel Graham hosted Bob and Jerry.

After their performance, the colonel escorted the entertainers back to the barracks. "Bet you're hungry after that long show," he said. "Want a sandwich?"

"Sure do," they answered.

"Then follow me back to the kitchen."

When they arrived, the colonel instructed them to tell the cooks what they wanted. After placing the order, Bob asked the cooks, "You fellows see the show?"

"No, sir, we couldn't. We had to stay here on duty."

Bob and Jerry stepped aside for a minute. They spoke with whispered tones. Then they asked, "Well, would you like to see the show *now?*"

Quite surprised, the soldiers replied, "Of course we would."

Then Bob Hope and Jerry Colonna performed the entire show, including the musical parts (minus the band).

In recounting the event, Colonel Graham told me, "I learned what true, dedicated entertainers Bob and Jerry were. Obviously, they considered an audience of any size worth their best effort."

Most of us have spoken to small audiences—sometimes disappointingly small. Deflated, we felt our enthusiasm disappearing. "This little group," we mused, "is hardly worth the effort."

I suggest keeping in mind the example Bob and Jerry set. Let's consider an audience of two or twenty just as significant as an audience of two thousand. Everyone who attends sets aside this time, looks forward to it, possibly pays a fee. These people anticipate our finest presentation. They deserve no less.

The most accomplished speakers care greatly about anyone willing to listen. And this is why audiences care about them.

ANALYZING YOUR AUDIENCE

IN ADDITION TO LEARNING AN IMPORTANT LESSON from Colonel Graham's story about Bob Hope, I learned another one by watching Bob in action. More than twenty years ago, I attended his show at the University of Georgia. As a faculty member in speech communication, I had special interest in his performance before a sell-out crowd.

The minute he opened his monologue, I knew he had sent an advance team to Athens (site of the university) to learn about the community. Bob mentioned local restaurants, night spots, and the Georgia "Bulldogs" football team. The audience roared when he asked his singer whether her perfume was named "Evening in Bogart." Bogart is a tiny town near Athens—not known for its exotic selection of fragrances.

Hope's show would have succeeded without these local references, I'm sure. But listeners, including me, appreciated his customized remarks. Please place this in your memory bank: *Customized speeches generate greater results than canned speeches.*

When you're going to give a speech, with ample head notice, there are several ways to analyze the group before you arrive.

Begin by asking your host for a membership booklet.

Browse the list, and you'll identify the professions represented. Now you can estimate the group's economic level, major interests, and concerns.

Request newsletters to learn about the organization's current activities. Notice community service, affiliations with charities, and accomplishments of individual members.

Check the Internet. For a national organization, you might locate a Web site, along with dozens of other entries—including articles about the local affiliate.

Talk with your host to evaluate your first impressions. Ask the host to provide a copy of the creed, motto, and statement of mission.

Your homework prepares you to select a relevant subject. Also, like Bob Hope, you're able to use illustrations listeners relate to and enjoy.

When the host introduces you to the audience, use your opening comments to establish rapport. For example: "It's a privilege to be with people who arc so concerned about this city's problems. I read about your highly successful project to improve the reading skills of public school children. Your president showed me the schedule of the teams who are visiting the schools and reading stories with students. I applaud your efforts wholeheartedly."

All successful speakers demonstrate familiarity with the audience. By following the steps I've suggested, you can do the same.

SPEECH PREPARATION METHODS

TO PREPARE AND DELIVER A SPEECH, YOU CAN select from four methods.

The **impromptu method** has the speaker giving a talk with no formal, structured preparation. The speaker relies on prior knowledge of the subject and speaks "off the cuff," as we say.

I can't recommend impromptu speaking when you have head notice. Too many things can go wrong—memory loss, excessive fear, rambling with no apparent direction, fumbling over simple statements, confusing the facts.

Of course, occasionally almost everyone hears the call to speak without warning. "Sally," the supervisor says, "tell the group about the convention you attended in Boston." No choice here!

Even while you're getting up from your chair, think of three or four topics you'll cover, such as the best session you attended, the convention theme, colleagues from your state who participated, and how you'll implement what you learned. Visualize key words which form your outline. Then give your report in conversational style.

You're aware, I'm sure, of the **manuscript method**. The speaker writes the speech, then relies on the text verbatim. Especially for novice speakers, manuscript speaking seems comforting. With every word chosen already, how can you miss?

Yet the tendency is for the speaker to rely too heavily on the script. Rather than speaking, we read the material—and sound like a reader. We use minimal eye contact, miss opportunities to observe audience reaction, and border on monotone delivery.

I recommend manuscript speaking only in circumstances when *exact wording is required.* Suppose your organization holds a press conference to answer questions about a fire, embezzlement, roof collapse, or accidental death. When the CEO presents her statement, she may not want to risk poor wording, since the wrong words invite lawsuits and insurance losses. But for ordinary speaking occasions, consider the manuscript a paper barrier between you and the audience.

A few speakers use the **memorization method**. Only a few people in a thousand succeed with this method. The pressure to memorize every word turns the speaker into an actor. Sure, stage veterans go beyond memorization, delivering lines with remarkable spontaneity. The rest of us resemble mannequins, who lip-synch someone else's words.

I recommend the **extemporaneous (or extemp) method**. The speaker researches the topic, then outlines thoroughly, relying on key words and phrases. Maybe she writes two or three sections (introduction, a long quotation, conclusion). But she concentrates on conveying the *key thoughts*, not the exact words.

The extemp speaker takes only a brief outline to the podium, glancing down occasionally to stay on track. Relieved of the obligation to follow a text exactly, either through reading or memorization, he addresses his audience with the cordial tone of a neighbor who dropped by to chat.

Honestly, I sympathize with speakers who cling to the text as though departure means death. I started out with that habit myself. Difficult as the switch was, I found freedom and joy when I faced audiences and gave a *talk* instead of an *essay*.

Try this: Envision a car salesman you're visiting for the third time. How many pages will he turn as he makes his closing appeal? Enough said.

LOOK MOM, NO NOTES!

WHEN WE WATCH SPEAKERS ADDRESS AN AUDIENCE without relying on any notes—sometimes leaving the podium to wander among the audience—we wonder how they do that. Do they have photographic memories? Do they just speak "off the cuff"?

Really, there's no mystery or magic here. Let's look behind the scenes.

One: The speaker doesn't think of the speech as a performance, as repetition of lines like those assigned to an actor. Rather, he considers the speech more like a *conversation.*

Remember your first speaking experience, probably in the eighth grade? In my class, we had to stand inside a chalk circle and speak for *exactly three minutes*. We wrote our speeches, memorized them—and stood there shaking, worried about the clock and our timing.

The accomplished speaker avoids that pressure, concentrating on sharing *ideas*—which generate far more animation than citing a script.

Two: The speaker operates from a high level of assurance because he has *a secret advantage over the audience.* The speaker knows what he *intends to say.* The audience has no clue about what's *supposed* to be said next.

What's the power of this advantage? The speaker relaxes, knowing he can leave out an example, a quotation, a statistic, or a personal incident without anybody being aware of the slipup.

Actually, the speaker won't label the omission a *mistake,* because he's not giving a performance graded on perfection. He's interacting with the audience, saying what fits at that moment.

Three: Take comfort in realizing the noteless speaker didn't get to that level overnight. Few people start out with poise of this caliber. Confidence increases with repetition, positive feedback from varied audiences, and gradual emancipation from note cards, pages, and manuscripts.

Four: The noteless speaker relies upon material that's *picturesque*. She doesn't remember the material, she *visualizes* it. Like a skilled novelist, she tells about real people in believable circumstances, people who often face great struggles, but overcome them with superlative courage and effort.

Think back to an exciting incident in your life. Maybe you'll recall an athletic event, an act of heroism, a frightening accident, meeting a celebrity, appearing on television for the first time, getting your driver's license, bringing a child home from the hospital, your big promotion, your first day as a college student, or comparable milestones in your life.

Do you need notes to tell me what happened, how you felt, what people said, what lessons you learned? I wouldn't think so.

The more your material *comes from within*, the freer you are to throw away mental props.

What do you think? Noteless speakers aren't doing what's impossible for the rest of us, are they?

Your turn comes next.

I SEE WHAT YOU MEAN

YOU'RE FAMILIAR WITH THE PHRASE "WORST-CASE scenario." Unfortunately, I have seen the phrase come to life when some speakers misuse visual aids.

Scenario number one: The speaker props a chart onto an easel, then says, "Probably those of you in the back of the room can't see this." Don't you assume, then, that she intends the display only for those who took seats in the front part of the room?

Find out the size of the room where you'll make your presentation. If the meeting room is local, go there several days ahead to determine how far away listeners might sit. Then prepare your chart, map, photos, or other visuals so they'll cover the distance.

Scenario number two: The speaker announces he'll show a videotape, then illustrates he can't work the equipment. Audience members grow restless, start talking—and leave the room mentally even if they remain in the room physically.

You're wise to try out the equipment *before* the audience arrives. Then if you stumble a few times, your efforts aren't embarrassing. Request extra light bulbs for slide projectors, extra batteries for specialized equipment. When possible, enlist a group member to operate the equipment—after you give adequate instruction.

Scenario number three: To show slides or overheads, the speaker dims the lights for her entire half-hour speech. Listeners nod off, as we're likely to do in a quiet, dark setting just after lunch.

Keeping the lights down presents another problem. After a few minutes, you're only a voice, which means you're forfeiting valuable nonverbal support—from gestures, facial expressions, posture, and mobility.

Also, in a dark room you miss what audience feedback could tell you. You wind up guessing the level of interest and comprehension—a rather risky venture.

Scenario number four: The speaker distributes a handout, then reads the material word for word. You wonder, "What is this—Literacy 101?"

Many accomplished presenters wait until *after* the speech to hand out information. Or they hand out only what they're discussing at that moment. And they *never* read verbatim an item the audience has in hand. Reading to adults comes across as an affront to their intelligence.

Considering how many other worst-case scenarios might occur, one highly successful speaker had this to say about visual aids: "No, Bill, I don't use them. Too many things can go wrong. A projector bulb blows, a slide sticks in the tray, or the print is too small."

His is an extreme view. My experience argues for the skilled use of visual aids. In the hands of a speaker who has planned and practiced, a prop illustrates, entertains, and educates. Who will forget O. J. Simpson's attempt to try on the pair of gloves in his first trial, and attorney Johnny Cochran's melodic charge, "If they don't fit, you must acquit"?

Select colorful, tasteful, relevant and visible visual aids, and your audience can truly say, "I see what you mean."

SURPRISE YOUR AUDIENCE

IN THE WASHINGTON HILTON HOTEL, I TOOK MY seat at the restaurant's breakfast counter. After taking my order, the waiter brought my coffee. So I turned to the lady beside me and asked, "Will you pass the cream, please?"

She answered, "No, I won't."

Naturally, I wondered if I had heard her wrong. That wasn't the routine answer. "Maybe," I said to myself, "I'm still groggy. It's early. Possibly I misunderstood her." For a reality check, again I asked her to pass the cream. This time, too, I included "please." Once more, she declined.

"Do you mind telling me why you won't pass the cream?"

"Sure," she said, without changing expression. "Because you expect me to. And now and then I like to surprise people who are so sure what I'm going to say and what I'm going to do."

For a minute, I pondered her statement. Then I commented, "Well, now that I know your motive, I commend you for being unique. You have surprised me—really surprised me. But the fact remains, I *still need the cream.* Will you pass it now?"

She slid the cream across the countertop to me, smiled, and wished me a good day.

More times than I can estimate, I've thought about that conversation. I'm convinced there's a message there for those who want to improve their speaking skills. Here it is: *Dare to try something out of the ordinary.*

Makes sense, particularly when we consider "the ordinary"—a shopworn joke to begin with, three main points, a highly structured outline, quotes from Mark Twain, Abe Lincoln, and John Kennedy. Expect, too, stories you've heard before.

No wonder audiences become jaded, anticipating boredom!

Surprise your audience. Display an unusual visual aid. Break into song in the middle of your speech (I couldn't get away with this . . . maybe you can. My audience would head for the exits by the third note.)

Speak five minutes when the audience expects twenty. A speaker did this at a Chamber of Commerce annual dinner.

Months later, audience members talked about the impact of his speech.

Arrange for a friend to interrupt your speech, and start debating you. Someone with decent acting skills will make the interruption look spontaneous.

Play a recording of "Hail to the Chief" as you approach the podium. You'll generate laughter before you say a word.

As long as you use good taste, you can grab attention in unforgettable fashion—just like the woman who told me she wouldn't pass the cream.

A MATTER OF TASTE

THE SPEAKER FACED HER AUDIENCE WITH A confident look. She seemed so poised that listeners expected a polished, highly professional job.

Unfortunately, within two minutes she lost her listeners. Why?

Not because she forgot her material. Not because she had trouble getting her words out—her enunciation was flawless and fluent. Not because she made inaccurate statements.

No, her problem arose when she used what we call, quite politely, "off-color" material. Thinking she was going to amuse us, she described her personal life with a man she was dating . . . in far greater detail than anyone wanted.

I can assure you, nobody laughed. I take that back—a few people laughed from discomfort and embarrassment. Most of us cringed and shuddered. We tuned out the rest of her talk.

Her speech reminded me of a civic-club incident. A guest speaker told a joke. A female member walked to the microphone, faced the audience, and said, "I consider this joke inappropriate for this group." She added, "I'm sure others share my opinion."

Then there was the speaker who delivered a college's baccalaureate address. Describing a disabled person, he provided ghastly details about her inability to control her bodily functions.

Here's the point: The speaker needs to illustrate high respect for the audience. Call this taste, decorum, judgment, or any comparable word. We must compliment our audience by assuming they want nothing less than dignified content.

Humor that draws a chuckle or laugh on the golf course or at a card table does not necessarily fit the speech setting. Intimate personal experiences are taboo. Boastful statements about your achievements, wealth, association with famous people, and honors will erect barriers you can't overcome.

As you plan a speech, and consider marginally acceptable material, have this piece of advice handy: *When in doubt . . . leave it out.*

ONCE UPON A TIME

HERE'S ONE OF THE PHRASES WE HEARD OFTEN during our childhood: "Once upon a time."

We liked to hear the phrase, because those words signaled that a story was on the way. The theme of the story didn't matter much. Whether someone was going to read to us about the Arabian nights, Snow White, or Red Ryder at Dry Gulch, we knew we were going to be entertained. Now and then, the story frightened us, but that was okay, because we were in a safe haven physically. Only our minds had wandered away, lured by heroism, mystical visions, even romance reaching far beyond our understanding.

Do we ever outgrow our love of good stories? I think not. Novelists know we don't. Movie producers—not all, but the best ones—are aware they have to include more than action and scenery. An intriguing plot is a must for maintaining attention.

Whenever you get an opportunity to speak to an audience, keep our affection for stories in mind. True, audiences can endure statistics, quotations, and a litany of complicated material . . . but not indefinitely. Break up those arid passages with a spellbinding story. They'll stay with you, wanting to know the outcome.

A speaker at my civic club portrayed the military careers of five World War II fighter pilots. He recounted their missions. By offering biographical sketches, he made them sound like the men next door in our neighborhoods. He described how some of the pilots became lifelong friends, and still enjoy reunions.

Frankly, he got by with inadequate visual aids (too small for all the audience to see) because his stories were so captivating. We became absorbed in the pictures he painted verbally.

You don't hear the phrase much now, but we used to refer to master storytellers as "raconteurs." Though the name has faded, the skill remains prominent. Probably you're aware of some speakers who specialize in storytelling, referring to themselves as storytellers and not as speakers.

I vote for abolishing the distinction. To achieve widespread success in speaking, you'll have to include forceful stories.

You can even relate stories in a stodgy business setting. Business and industry people love stories. How else could we explain the popularity of "roasts," when even fictional stories enliven the evening? Usually the true ones amuse us, too, and deepen our appreciation for the individual we're honoring.

Any professional speaker will verify these guidelines. Stories have to be credible, ethically acceptable, and fresh enough not to be trite. The best stories make a point, and often underscore a moral standard. Our senses and imaginations become ultra active.

No, you're not likely to begin with "Once upon a time." Yet "An interesting thing happened to me last week" will bring on the same magic we felt as very young listeners.

LET ME SPEAK TO YOU FOR A MINUTE

THE CHAMBER OF COMMERCE'S SPECIAL LUNCH meeting offered a unique networking opportunity for forty professional people.

Unique? In what way? Networking groups gather daily, especially with Chambers of Commerce. Participants swap business cards, describe products and services, and seek appointments.

Well, what set apart this glad-handing occasion was the time limitation. Each guest spoke to the entire group for sixty seconds, with no overtime allowed. The chamber executive acted as timekeeper, and he allowed no latitude.

Sixty seconds. Why, most opening jokes last that long. How could anybody profile his or her business that quickly?

The results astounded all of us. Each speaker adjusted to the restriction. Some even quit a few seconds early.

Afterward, most of us could have identified each speaker's profession. We gravitated toward those whose presentations interested us most.

As a former university speech professor, my mind started toying with how the working world would change if all presenters had to conform to the one-minute regulation.

Imagine a university prof restricted to one minute daily for each class. (Somehow, fifty minutes became sacrosanct years ago.) Obviously five or six habitual late-coming students might not hear a word all semester. And with so little said, the bookstore would face serious budget deficits, considering the drop in sales of notebooks.

How about politicians? "Senator, we need your opinion about the coeducational training of recruits in the armed services." By the time the respondent got through explaining "the two sides to the issue," the gong would sound.

Picture a one-minute sales pitch in answer to "Why should we hire you for this project?" We'd miss the salesperson's latest jokes, athletic scores and stories, weather report, and questions about our family.

And what would happen to religious services? The speaker could read one verse of holy writ, assure us that a divine being loves us, forgives us, and wants us to help one another—then announce the benediction (a short one, at that). No time for poems, no relating of testimonials.

The newscaster could merely report: "Today there were two robberies, one fire, three traffic jams, and the stock market rose." Thirty seconds of national headlines would follow.

Gosh, no joking among the news team, no interviewing of witnesses, no mayor's statement.

Personally, as I consider these drastic changes, I believe the sixty-second rule might improve our speechmaking. If it didn't, though, as listeners we'd only lose a minute per speech.

HAVE SPEECH, WILL TRAVEL

YOU LOOK AT THE CONFERENCE PROGRAM. THE first morning's session opens with a keynote speaker. Browsing through the next three days, you find other speakers and workshop leaders listed. You wonder who these people are. So many people avoid giving speeches . . . and here are men and women who choose to do this for a living.

What's their motivation? How about their qualifications? Do they give the same speech everywhere?

Because I'm a professional speaker and trainer, I can report from my own experience, and the experiences of other members of the National Speakers Association.

People become professional speakers because they have a message they want to share with a large public. Customarily, the message has evolved from their life experiences. Something has worked for them, so they're convinced the same beliefs and lifestyles will work for others.

The speakers with the greatest impact, the speakers who last in this profession, do more than believe in a message. They believe *passionately.* You'll see and hear an evangelistic fervor when they take the stage.

Dick Biggs, a fellow resident of Gainesville, Georgia, talks about his "Optimum Living System," which he describes in his book, *If Life Is a Balancing Act, Why Am I So Darn Clumsy?* He emphasizes balancing our priorities. Twenty years ago, he didn't know about that. He was a college dropout, experienced a divorce, and tried several jobs that brought only partial satisfaction. Now he's a happy husband and father, with a host of friends and strong values. In his presentations, he encourages others to find out *what's really important.*

Change Your Communication—Change Your Life!

Aspiring speakers run the risk of concentrating too heavily on how to deliver speeches. Of supreme importance, for both the occasional speaker and the full-time professional, is having a message which changes attitudes and action.

Regarding qualifications, a number of speakers and trainers were professional communicators before they joined the speaking circuit—radio and television broadcasters, sales trainers, teachers, and public relations staff members. I started my career as a speech communication faculty member at the University of Georgia.

I mentioned the National Speakers Association. The association is neither honorary nor all-inclusive. Joining requires documentation of speeches given to audiences—with the hosting organizations paying for the speaker's services.

Again, an individual becomes a professional speaker because of a personal commitment to continuing education. We're delighted to work with corporations and associations who are willing to invest in personnel development. Besides labeling ourselves *motivators*, we're proud to be considered *educators*.

Do speakers give just one speech, with only the faces of the listeners changing? While the major thrust remains the same, we *customize* our content for each audience. The professional speaker doesn't speak "to whom it may concern." He or she speaks to this audience, this day, at this time. Even sticking with the traditional theme, top-level speakers spend many hours preparing to meet *the needs of this audience*.

Frankly, the speakers I know wouldn't want to become mere reciters, mimicking what they said yesterday. They thrive on a *live* audience, with dynamic interaction visibly, emotionally, and often vocally.

A final comment about professional speakers: We know that having you in our audience is a privilege we should never take lightly. Our greatest reward—far more stimulating than publicity, applause, and warm handshakes at the door—is finding out we said something valuable for your everyday living.

6

LISTENING

IN 1957, DR. RALPH NICHOLS WROTE A BOOK ENTITLED *Are You Listening?* drawing attention to an oft-neglected fact: successful communication requires competent *receivers* as well as *senders*.

In a typical day, we could hear these comments:

"What was your name again, please?"

"Did you say you wanted your food to go?"

"Sorry, I missed your order. Will you please give it to me again?"

"Oh, you said you're from Milwaukee. I thought you said Miami."

"What did you say—you'll pay by cash or charge card?"

One thing for sure—we don't want to *make* those comments, or give similar signs of inadequate listening. Nonlisteners lose sales, friendships, even family relationships.

Become a number one listener . . . and you'll climb to the top of everybody's list.

A LINGERING LESSON

PICTURE A HOT AUGUST DAY IN SOUTH MISSISSIPPI. The scene: a feed, seed, and fertilizer warehouse.

I'm working there as a fifteen year old, the first of several summers unloading freight trains, and eventually putting those heavy sacks into customers' trucks.

One of my co-workers tells me, "Bill, things seem sorta slow here. Think you can handle the place for an hour while the rest of us go to lunch?"

"Sure, go right ahead," I answered. After all, I was fifteen years old. At that age, you're not going to say you can't do something.

"Want us to bring you anything?"

"Yeah. Hamburger, no onions. Bag of chips, too. And I'll just get a coke from our machine."

Within half a minute after they turned the corner, a pickup truck backed up to the ramp. I rose, stood as tall as I could, and ambled to the edge of the loading dock.

"Howdy, sir, can I help you?"

"Yep," he said blandly, and he told me his order. Then he handed me the scribbled confirmation that showed he had paid at the store's office.

"Be back in a minute," I said, as I got one of the upright delivery carriers we called "dollies." I wheeled the dolly to the back of the warehouse, stopping at a huge stack of 5/10/5 fertilizer—so named because each number indicated the percentage of certain ingredients.

I had two choices. Needing to load ten sacks, I could do two loads of five sacks, or one load with all ten stacked on the dolly. We're talking about 100 pound sacks, so taking the full order would mean wheeling half a ton at once. Here again, the bravado of youth won out. I loaded all ten fertilizer sacks.

I reached his truck a little winded, but had enough energy to lift and drop the sacks onto the back of his truck. Strangely, he never said a word. He just stood there with his hands in his overalls. A wide straw hat shielding his face kept me from seeing his expressions.

The sound of sack number ten landing in the truck satisfied me greatly. Wiping the sweat from my face, I managed to conceal the pride I felt. Combining a slight swagger with a wide smile, I asked: "Anything else, sir?"

"Yep, there is boy. You can take 'em all back."

"Take 'em all back? What do you mean?"

"I said to take 'em all back. I didn't order ten *sacks* of 5/10/5. I ordered ten *pounds.*"

Crestfallen, I reread the crumpled order slip and saw he was right. Mumbling a feeble, forced apology, I emptied his truck. Then I brought him the ten pounds he needed.

"Sonny," he said, "right now you may hate me for letting you throw those heavy sacks down into my truck. But I'm just ornery enough to believe you'll listen to instructions a lot more carefully from now on before you start a job."

He was right about my anger. I was burning with rage. I felt the blood throbbing in my temples, and I was too short of breath to answer. My impulse was to tell him off. Somehow, I restrained myself.

He was right, too, about teaching me a memorable lesson. Never again have I listened to instructions carelessly. Always, I give total attention . . . remembering the pickup truck, and the cunning customer who drove it on that blazing day.

The farmer's lesson has helped me when I've heard instructors give assignments, taken travel directions, had weekly meetings with bosses, and listened to prospective clients describe their needs. Really, the instances are too numerous to mention.

You're long gone now, old farmer. Yet your lesson in listening helps me get orders right the first time.

LISTENING—A KEY COMPONENT OF LEADERSHIP

THE INTERVIEW PARTY INCLUDED TYPICAL CHITCHAT. "How did the house hunting go today?" the CEO asked.

We described the one we had selected, and he commented, "Good choice. You'll like that area."

Then we talked about favorite vacation spots, children, golf, and similar topics.

When we shifted to business, the CEO told me, "Your contract letter is at your hotel." Clearly, the job was mine.

Three interview trips had brought us to this stage.

The dinner lasted well into the evening. As we headed for the door, my would-be-boss asked, "Well, did you find a house today?"

Those words stunned me. Somehow, our earlier remarks had bypassed him. He hadn't listened—even to information he had requested.

The next morning, my wife and I rehashed the incident. "If this man missed something so simple," I wondered, "would he listen to my problems at work?"

"Probably not," she answered. "If last night gave a sample of his listening habits, he wouldn't support you as an employee."

We tore up the job offer, headed for the car, and sent a letter of decline the following day. Years later, we feel sure about our decision. The man wasn't a leader.

Leaders listen to a confused employee. They ask, "How can I clarify those instructions for you?"

Leaders listen to suggestions for improvement. They welcome feedback: "You've made a valuable recommendation, one nobody else thought of."

Leaders listen to family concerns: "I know your spouse's illness weighs heavily on your mind. Please update me about her progress."

Leaders listen to complaints: "You say our expectations are unreasonable? Give me an example."

During his fifty years as CEO of a department store, my father detested making speeches. He declined many invitations. Yet he maintained high credibility through his skills as a listener. Employees and customers confided in him frequently.

Yes, the genuine leader listens sincerely. I wouldn't tear up a contract that person offers.

LISTENING AND MORALE

IN BUSINESS AND INDUSTRY CIRCLES, THERE'S A well-known true story about an attempt to improve employee morale in an industrial plant. Top managers had become aware of growing unrest, even resentment. Workers appeared bored, uninspired. Supervisors couldn't identify the working conditions that caused morale to drop.

The logical action, managers agreed, was to make some environmental changes until attitudes improved visibly.

The first step was to ask workers about the lighting. With the required tasks dependent upon adequate illumination, maybe dark assembly lines caused the disgruntlement. Inspectors gathered opinions and asked for suggestions. Then changes came—more bulbs here, larger bulbs there, new angles for the light to shine onto equipment.

Attention turned next to the dining area. What did employees say about the cafeteria? Was the food tasty? Did the chef vary the menu frequently enough? How about value—was there enough food on the plates to justify prices? Were lunch lines too long, allotted times for eating too brief?

Next, supervisors quizzed employees about work breaks. Were they given fairly? Was the break room comfortable? Were breaks happening at the right time of day?

For weeks, the surveys, the inspections, and the changes continued. Simultaneously, employee morale climbed . . . and kept climbing. Workers shed their glum looks and put on cheerful faces. Complaints diminished, along with absenteeism.

With the changes completed, managers wanted to know *which change had been most responsible for generating better attitudes*. To find out, they called in a cross-section of employees—and put the question to them directly: "Tell us, please. Which improvement was most important to you and those around you? Brighter lights, better food, more parking spaces, or others—we'd like to know which improvement made the biggest difference."

The answer startled the managers. "Oh, none of those particularly stands out. The reason you're seeing happier people here at the plant is simple. *You asked us what we thought, and listened to us. What we said seemed to matter. Up until recently, we hadn't experienced that responsiveness to our opinions and needs.*"

Whether we're dealing with an individual or a group, we'll stimulate morale by listening intently to the needs of others. Sometimes, our attentiveness carries more value than our actions.

CRITICAL LISTENING

WHEN I USE THE TERM "CRITICAL LISTENING," "critical" does not imply cynical, fault-finding listening. My intent is to encourage receivers of messages to *critique* what they hear. Critique allows both positive and negative evaluations. The critical listener, then, guards against fraud and deception, cutting through propaganda to find substance.

What thought patterns relate to critical listening?

First: You examine the general assumption the presenter wants you to accept.

Suppose an educator says, "No child should waste time watching television." Accept that premise, and you'll exclude educational television from a child's mental development.

I'll bet you've heard even more bizarre allegations, such as "The holocaust is just a hoax thought up by a few people" and "There was no walk on the moon. NASA filmed those scenes in the desert." Allow them to go unquestioned, and demagogues will enjoy a head start with mind control.

Second: With critical listening, you examine the evidence thoroughly.

When a television advertisement claims "three out of four doctors recommend this product," clear-thinking listeners will ask, "Does the sponsoring company pay them for their testimony? How large was the group of physicians—four or four thousand?"

Also, how recent is the evidence? Outdated supporting material loses validity.

Third: Examine the communicator's credibility.

In the above illustration about endorsements, ask: "When we say 'doctor,' are we referring to M.D.'s? If so, what's their specialty? Are they board certified in the specialty? Are they engaged in practice? Have they maintained solid reputations?"

Critical listening will protect us from those who operate on half-truths, innuendos, name-calling and other persuasive attempts which ignore rational decision making.

LIVELY LISTENING

IN OUR CHILDHOOD, PARENTS, TEACHERS AND OTHER authority figures taught us to listen passively. We heard "Don't interrupt," "Wait your turn," "Let the other person finish," "Silence is golden," "Be seen and not heard." At that stage, the instruction made sense. Children must learn to curb the impulse to dominate conversation.

However, adults need a different concept of listening. The adult role requires moving beyond silent, passive reception. With "lively listening," we assume responsibility for *facilitating dialogue*.

Let's compare conversation to acting. In a play or movie, performers talk when they hear "cue lines" from others. Audiences assume the words and action are spontaneous, but, of course we know they aren't. In *Gone with the Wind,* Rhet answered Scarlett's cues, and she answered his.

In college, I acted in a play that bordered on disaster, because a fellow actor forgot his lines. He stumbled, improvised, wandered, and stammered through most of one scene. The entire cast got confused (and yes, frightened) because we didn't hear our cues. Amazingly, we kept the play moving until the bewildered actor remembered his part.

What's the point? This: When someone talks with you, either in a professional, social, or family setting, the conversation gains energy and meaning when you provide cues for the speaker. The speaker welcomes your *lively listening*, and becomes more animated. You enter a partnership.

In your next conversation, try cue lines like these:

"That's very interesting."

"Hmmmm, tell me more."

"And then what happened?"

"I see."

"Sounds like you had a very frustrating day."

"I'm not sure I understand what you just said."

Believe me, people will say you're a person they love to talk with—because you prompt *them* to talk.

PHYSICIANS AS LISTENERS

FOR MORE THAN THIRTY YEARS, D. B. CONERLY JR., M.D., practiced surgery in Hattiesburg, Mississippi. Because he's my brother-in-law, I've enjoyed opportunities to talk with him about the central role of communication in a physician's practice.

"Bill," he said as we paused between golf shots, "I've seen surgeons who knew all they needed to know about the technical side of medicine, and whose skills in the operating room generated admiration from their colleagues. But some of them still failed to provide an acceptable level of patient care."

When I asked Dr. Conerly what was missing in their surgical practice, he answered quickly that "they are weak on diagnosis. And the reason is simple. They don't listen to patients when patients try to describe their symptoms."

"The surgeons I have in mind," he explained, "aren't willing to hear *everything the patient can tell them.* After one or two sentences, these surgeons decide what's wrong—and schedule treatment."

Dr. Conerly lamented the missed opportunities. "The patient could really help the doctor with the diagnosis. The patient can say exactly what's wrong, if the doctor will just let the patient finish talking."

Having experienced several surgeries, I have been fortunate enough to select surgeons who exemplified the good listening Dr. Conerly advocates.

Dr. Conerly spends much of his retirement time as a sought-after speaker, addressing groups about hospice and alcoholism—the latter subject resulting from his personal recovery several years ago. As much as I respect his speaking talent, I'm more grateful for his recognition of the significance of listening in the healing process.

THE LISTENER'S ULTIMATE CHALLENGE

LONG-WINDED TALKERS PRESENT SEVERE PROBLEMS for listeners. I've come across many of them, and I'm sure you have as well.

There was Cousin Sally. Sally had many wonderful attributes. She loved her family and friends. She took special interest in young people. Her smile was genuine and captivating.

Unfortunately, she mastered the art of monologue. She could take the simplest event and expand her description into epic proportions. At family reunions, when the time came to take our seats at the dinner table, relatives scrambled madly to avoid the chair next to hers. Even now, her nonstop chatter remains vivid in memory.

There was the retired person who responded to the question, "What were some of the highlights of your career?" After one hour of giving more details than any listener would want, he had advanced only until 1934. His guest stood, mentioned another appointment, and walked out the door—exasperated and exhausted.

If you and I were enjoying a conversation now, you'd be able to describe a few champion chatterboxes yourself.

How does a listener deal with these talkers who expect 100 percent attention?

In a few cases, you might succeed by giving nonverbal cues—looking at your watch, standing and moving toward the door, shifting eye contact to items on your desk, or gathering your materials and placing them in your briefcase.

Yet these signals mean nothing to the most addicted talkers. They'll follow you to the parking lot and keep talking after you've cranked your car.

In her book *That's Not What I Meant,* Dr. Deborah Tannen gives this advice for dealing with compulsive talkers: *Adapt to their communication style, and use an identical style in responding.*

Ordinarily, to honor what parents taught us about etiquette, we employ a passive style. Feeling overwhelmed, we relinquish control entirely. What happens? The talker stays in charge. And stays in charge, ad infinitum (and ad nauseam, to be candid).

Tannen proposes playing their game. We won't offend them, because they acknowledge interruption as an acceptable step in conversing. Soon we'll have our say, which we wouldn't have otherwise.

Another recommendation: When you're scheduled to meet with a verbose colleague, choose their office, not yours. You'll have an easier time exiting their place than you would moving them from yours.

When your office is the only choice, as with an external visitor, try this: "I'm so happy you came by. I have twenty minutes allotted for us. How can I help you?"

No, we're not likely to *cure* big-league talkers. We can, though, employ subtle, courteous means of *control.*

7

TELEPHONE

ON MARCH 10, 1876, ALEXANDER GRAHAM BELL spoke these words to his assistant: "Mr. Watson, come here, I want you." A simple statement, of course—but the words made history, because with this message Bell demonstrated that his new invention, the telephone, could transmit sound across distances.

Bell died in 1922. He lived long enough to see his invention transform personal and commercial communication. Think, though, of how amazed he would be to witness the omnipresence of the telephone today—car phones, phones we carry to the swimming pool, phones in hotel bathrooms, phones for golf carts!

He'd shake his head in bewilderment and amazement over answering services, answering machines, teleconferencing, call waiting, automatic redial—and a host of other expansions to the simple set he built.

While we have been making technical improvements, have we kept pace in training people for *proper use of the telephone?* I'll let you answer the question. Think of the last dozen calls you've placed or received. Did the other parties use good judgment . . . and good manners? You're unusually lucky if more than half of them did.

How do you rate yourself as a phone partner?

Read on—and design your next calls accordingly.

FAMILY TRADITION

A S MUCH AS I APPRECIATE HOW E-MAIL, FAX, NEXT-day mail delivery, and chat rooms allow us to get in touch quickly, I haven't found any method as personal and heart-warming as an old-fashioned telephone call.

My family perpetuates a tradition started by my parents a generation ago. When I went to college, my father and mother called me every Sunday night, to see what had gone on during the week, and to wish me well for the next week. Those calls reminded me of my roots. Daddy and Mother shared family news and updates about my hometown. Our conversations helped me through exams, fraternity rush, changing majors, career decisions, and dating problems.

We maintained the habit—which was well on the way to becoming a tradition—after my marriage. I recall vividly two or three times when my wife, Sandra, and I would miss their call, because we were out for the evening or hadn't returned from a trip. All of us felt a void.

Not surprisingly, we established the Sunday calling habit with her parents, too. Even now, we call her mother—the one remaining link with our immediate ancestry—before or after her church and bridge game.

We're continuing the tradition with our children. For years, we've called our daughters on Sunday nights—first at college, then in the homes they established as wives. If any of us has plans for Sunday evening, we call early in the day.

Sometimes Sandra and I place the calls, sometimes the daughters do. Nobody keeps score. What's important is that we talk at a day and time we have come to cherish.

Throughout the week, both daughters communicate with us by e-mail. Phone calls happen on weeknights, too. Yet the expectation for a Sunday family call remains. Hearing the phone on Sunday evening, I'm likely to comment: "Must be Suzanne. We've talked with Shelley already."

We've reached the stage where much of the conversation revolves around grandchildren—the first day of school, summer activities, new playmates, doctor visits, accomplishments, funny comments, birthday plans—and on occasions when they're not playing video games and are in the mood to say hello, we'll talk to Collin, Megan, and Jay.

Everybody wants to leave a legacy. Years from now, one of mine will take place on Sundays, when my children call their children. They'll talk with them the same way all of us have talked:

"Hi. How was your week?"

"Oh, let me tell you about. . . ."

WHERE'S THE GOAL?

FOOTBALL FANS REMEMBER THE 1929 ROSE BOWL game, featuring the University of California against Georgia Tech, for staging one of football's unforgettably bizarre plays. One of UC's defensive players, Roy Riegel, picked up a Georgia Tech fumble and headed for the goal line. The problem was, he got confused in the excitement—and headed toward his own end zone, not Georgia Tech's.

Riegel mistook the crowd noise for applause. When one of his California teammates tried to stop him, Riegel thought the player just wanted to take the ball, to get personal credit for the six points. Annoyed, Riegel yelled, "This is my touchdown!"

He crossed the goal line. Georgia Tech tackled him for a safety, and scored two points. Those points allowed Tech to post the 8 to 7 winning score.

Riegel achieved lifelong fame, of the dubious sort. Many years later his private plane became temporarily lost.

Headlines reported, "Wrong Way Riegel Lost Again."

Apply Riegel's mistake to telephone conversations you have heard. You decide the caller suffers from the Riegel malady, not knowing where the goal is. The conversation runs this way, then that, without identifiable purpose. Callers who seem lost frustrate us. We look at our watches, and try to think of excuses to end the aimless chatter. More often than not, we daydream, so the caller wastes his time and ours.

Effective telephone calls require preparation. Please understand, I'm not recommending scripted conversations. Several times a week, you confront telemarketers who illustrate the deadliness of "canned" calls. The caller becomes a reader, and not a very interesting one.

I recommend *listing the major points you intend to make.* Purposely, I avoided the word *outlined.* An outline tends to reveal *too much structure*, which inhibits free-flowing dialogue. The list I have in mind is nothing more than key words and phrases.

Let's say you're phoning a community leader to get her involved in a Chamber of Commerce project to reduce illiteracy. You want the person to attend an orientation session, then agree to help tutor children two afternoons a month after school. Your key word outline reads:

Chamber
Illiteracy
Orientation
Tutoring

With this list before you, you *know your goal.* Immediately, the listener recognizes you are aware of your direction. The listener attends to your message patiently, welcoming your forethought that conserves time and fosters comprehension.

Often I preview the goal as soon as we finish the rapport stage. "Ted," I'll say, "I'll appreciate just a couple of minutes of your time now, so I can tell you about an exciting project sponsored by the Chamber of Commerce."

As listeners, we have the right to ask for a goal statement when the caller fails to mark the direction for us. Here's how to get the conversation on track:

"How can I help you today?"

"I'm not sure what you have in mind. Can you give me some clarification, please?"

"What involvement are you asking me to agree to?"

"I may have missed your main point. Will you please give me a quick summary?"

Use one of these questions the next time you get a Roy Riegel call.

SURVIVING VOICE MAIL

A PROFESSIONAL COLLEAGUE I HAD MET CALLED me at my office two weeks afterward. I gave my usual greeting: "Hello, this is Bill Lampton." No one commented. After a few seconds, the woman laughed—energetically. I wondered if my greeting caused her lively outburst.

"Bill," she said after identifying herself, "I'm sorry. It's just that I haven't heard *a real person answer the phone* in so long, you startled me!"

You can understand her surprise. Frequently, in place of the real-live person, we get a recording. Then we're challenged to think quickly, possibly make a selection from up to ten choices (each of which might lead to other selections), and record a message when the beep gives the signal.

Voice mail generates special frustration for people who began using telephones several decades ago, particularly in small towns. To ring a number, they'd pick up the phone and an operator would answer with "Number, please." The caller gave the number. The operator would let the call ring several times, then say, "Sorry, no one is there now" when nobody answered. Or she'd tell you, "That line is busy. Try again, please." Or you'd connect successfully, and the operator left the line (you hoped).

In smaller communities, operators chatted with callers while calls were connecting. "Didn't I see your college daughter home for the holidays?" was not considered meddling—just friendly interest.

Imagine going from *high touch* to *high tech* in a relatively short span. However, even people who never experienced highly personalized phone assistance balk at voice mail.

Some of us attempt to enliven our voice-mail recordings with humor. When I called a banking association in Washington, my intended talker's voice mail came on with this message:

> *I can tell by your call you're looking for Bob,*
> *Who in this office does a heckuva job*
> *But you will know by this little tune*
> (Here the music background became much louder)
> *That I won't be back until after noon.*

When Bob and I talked later, I applauded his creativity.

Then there was Jack's recording. I reached Jack by accident, by dialing the wrong area code. Yet I'm glad I made the mistake, for his voice mail informed me:

> *Hello, this is Jack. Welcome to voice mail hell!*

Certainly everyone who leaves a recording has to decide how far to go with humor without sacrificing professional dignity. Ask yourself: What if my best prospect called? The client who gives me the most business? An angry customer? The board chairman? My supervisor?

Consider as well the nature of your service. I'd advise funeral homes and similarly somber organizations to avoid comical messages.

As with any communication message, change the recording regularly. Include your company's motto every time if you wish, but assure variety by using different greetings and sign-offs, and possibly different quotes or thoughts for the day.

Even when humor doesn't greet me, I've come to appreciate the value of voice mail. Not long ago I agreed to make twenty-six phone calls to promote attendance at a Georgia

Speakers Association meeting. I agreed to do so under one condition—that I could leave messages for those I missed, without worrying about return calls. My choice was a good one. I reached only eight of those on my list. The others heard my meeting reminder through voice mail. Getting the word to this group would have consumed far more time if I had chatted with each person personally.

My suggestions for leaving messages:

State your name at the beginning and end of the message, including your phone number at the end. Even if the person has your number already, you're making a callback easier, and thus more likely.

Don't worry about a *perfect* recording. This isn't broadcasting, and you're not auditioning for a role. If you stammer and stumble, so what? We do that with other presentations. Chances are, your listener will barely notice.

Keep your message short. A busy friend told me that when he's out of town he spends at least half an hour a day listening to his recorded messages. Surely he welcomes those who say what's needed without extra words.

You have every right to leave a second message when your first one prompts no response. In this case, try: "Hello, I'm just calling to say I'm still eager to get in touch with you. I know you're very busy. I think we can keep our conversation to five minutes when you find an opportunity to call. I'll appreciate hearing from you."

FIVE THINGS YOU DON'T WANT TO HEAR WHEN YOU CALL

SOMEBODY ANSWERS THE PHONE AT THE OFFICE you dialed. The person you want to speak to isn't available. You say you want to leave a message. The reply: "Sure, now let me just find something to write with." You hear papers shuffling, drawers opening and shutting, a loud sigh, and then, "I know there's a pencil here somewhere." After much wasted time, the person says, "All right, I've got something now. What's your message, please?"

First: On my list of comments that offend me during phone conversations, the above rank at the top. A person with phone responsibilities *knows* the likelihood of being asked to relay messages. The person *knows* to write these down, unless they're put on voice mail. The person *knows* that to write, a writing instrument and paper are required. Then why, I want to ask in exasperation, doesn't the answering party have the writing equipment *within arm's length?*

Pen (or pencil, who cares?) are essential tools for noting messages. To not know where they are makes my mind go through these imagined scenes:

You're fading away under anesthetic. The surgeon enters the room. He starts searching the instrument table. He says to the operating staff, "I'm sure there's a scalpel here somewhere."

You show up for your tennis lesson. The instructor meets you at the court. He's carrying a can of tennis balls. He asks, "Has anybody seen a racquet around here?"

You go to a night football game, arriving as darkness falls. The announcer tells the crowd, "The game will start in fifteen minutes. But we aren't sure where the light switch is."

Ludicrous situations? Of course . . . because in each case vital equipment was missing—equipment *required* for functioning. Yet these hypothetical instances are no less zany than the person who *thinks* there's something to write with.

Second: "I don't think that person is here now." I'll interpret that several ways, with all of them negative. The speaker isn't alert enough to know who's there and who isn't. The person I asked about doesn't keep staff informed. The person I wanted is there, but has left instructions to stall callers. The person left instructions not to take *my* call. I don't care whether the answering party *thinks* the person is there. I just want the facts, not opinions.

I recommend substitute statements, such as a noncommittal, "Just a moment, please." You're familiar, I'm sure, with other ways to buy time as you search for the requested individual.

Third: "I have to get off the phone now. I have an important call I have to take." Really, now! Then what are you saying about the call you're ending—the one with me?

Without being offended, I'll accept: "Bill, there's an emergency I have to handle that has just come to my attention. I'll take care of it, and call you right back." I don't mind moving down the pecking order during a crisis.

Fourth: We don't want to hear continued conversations as the person prepares to speak with us. I'm all for a convivial work setting. Camaraderie reduces tension, as does humor. However, when the phone rings, the sound signals us to literally place current chitchat on hold. The call takes priority—*exclusively*. The preparation stage needs to happen during the two rings prior to answering. I want undivided attention, with the human connection simultaneous with the electronic connection.

Fifth: "I'll put you on hold." Convenient for the recipient, maybe, but not for me. Unless I'm waiting for someone who's almost impossible to reach, and this is my one chance for several weeks, I consider holding a waste of time. If I want three minutes of music, I'll turn on the radio . . . and select the station myself.

The more appropriate procedure is, "Do you mind holding for a minute, please?" The caller deserves the choice.

How strong are my opinions on this point? Well, if it weren't for my family, I know my tombstone would have this inscription: *I'm still on hold!*

KEEPING TRACK OF THOSE PHONE NOTES

THE PHONE RINGS. BY HABIT, YOU GRAB A PIECE OF paper and pen. Within seconds, you're glad you did. This is your supervisor, calling from out of town. You take notes rapidly. As the call nears conclusion, you summarize aloud what you've written, to make sure you heard the information correctly. The boss commends you for your thoroughness. When the call ends, you go to lunch.

Returning from lunch, you find a stack of new reports on your desk. You're not surprised, because they arrive on Tuesdays without fail. To make room for them, you clear your desk—cramming some items into a desk drawer, others into space in the credenza. You attack the reports energetically.

The next morning you pull out your calendar. You see this notation, made at closing time yesterday: "Follow supervisor's instructions." No problem—because you took those good notes during the phone conversation.

You open the desk drawer, confident you'll locate the piece of paper quickly. You see other familiar pages, but not the one you want. You get an idea. "Oh, the credenza. I put some stuff there, too." Once more, the same searching process. Another blank.

"Maybe I accidentally threw the information away," you muse, by now quite flustered. You look into the wastebasket, only to find that housekeeping made the morning rounds before you arrived. Empty . . . just like the feeling in your stomach.

You ask your assistant, "Did I give you my summary of yesterday's phone conversation? Did you file it?" Again, disappointment.

What to do? Go from memory? No, too many important details. Call and admit you misplaced the notes? You'd look too careless. None of your choices are good ones.

You go home dejected. Rather casually, your spouse remarks, "Before going to the cleaners this morning, I emptied your coat pockets. You left a piece of paper there. I put it on your reading table."

Hopefully, you pick up the page. Yes, *there* are those notes. For the first time in hours, you breathe again. And you vow this won't happen again.

Have I described frantic moments you've experienced? Then I'll join you in anguished memories. I've been there many times.

For years, I grabbed any paper item on my desk—used envelopes, memo pads, sticky notes, the company's newsletter. I used no system for placing those notations. Frequently, I suffered through the embarrassment, frustration, and waste of time described above.

One day I was browsing through the school supply section of a drugstore. I saw a simple spiral notebook, with 150 lined sheets. A light bulb went off in my brain. *What would happen if I kept every phone note there, removing pages only for filing purposes?*

The following day, I initiated my new method. Old habits die hard, and several times I fumbled for bits of paper nearest to my right hand. Catching myself, I reached for the notebook instead. The story has a happy ending. I have eliminated the distractions that accompany misplaced messages.

Consider these helpful guidelines, too. Write only one message per page. You'll use more paper, but you'll simplify filing. Date each page. In follow-up efforts, you'll say, "Going back to our phone conversation on June 14 . . ."

Every couple of months, I buy one of those spiral notebooks. They're worth far more than I spend. Without hesitation, I'll purchase tranquility and efficiency for a couple of dollars, anytime.

8

COMPUTERS

WHEN I TELL NEW ACQUAINTANCES I'M IN THE communication business, many assume I'm referring to computers. That's understandable, because computers have become a dominant fixture in our communication activities. Almost one third of Americans now "go on line," with that number expanding by millions annually.

Although I know very little about the technical aspects of computers (it took me awhile to learn how to scan, defragment, and operate an antivirus program), my daily reliance upon the Internet prompts me to offer observations that will help other novices become competent and comfortable in cyberspace.

LIVING HAPPILY WITH E-MAIL

E-MAIL (SHORT FOR ELECTRONIC MAIL) FASCINATES those of us who spent many years relying on "snail mail." (Remember letters, envelopes, and stamps—still necessary, but far more infrequent now?)

I marvel that I can type a business message on my computer screen, punch a button, and have those words appear on a client's screen hundreds of miles away, almost instantly. The reply may come quicker than I could have addressed an envelope.

Or if the client doesn't read my morning message until midnight, and answers then, I can read the answer at my convenience—even when I travel.

E-mail has brought many grandparents into computer training classes. They want to use this easy, fun way to keep in touch with their children and grandchildren.

In addition to business and family usage, e-mail opens channels to strangers. Internet chat rooms operate through e-mail. And when you admire someone's Web site, you become acquainted through e-mail.

Not only is e-mail quick and convenient, it's inexpensive. Unlike fax and long distance telephone calls, one monthly fee covers unlimited e-mail use. As long as this arrangement lasts, we have one of the greatest bargains imaginable.

To utilize e-mail wisely, remember that your messages are not confidential. A manager at Pillsbury criticized company executives in an e-mail to a colleague. His supervisor fired him. The released employee sued, claiming invasion of privacy. The court rejected his argument, declaring that the company has a right to see what's written on company time and equipment. The case is not exceptional. Big brother is watching—and has access to what you think you have erased.

Someone told me, "Don't put anything on e-mail you don't want displayed on an interstate highway billboard." So refrain from sending messages with personnel information, either good or bad. Be aware that gossip or love notes might terminate a job quickly.

Also, assume your readers will have greater likelihood of misinterpreting written messages. Spoken language furnishes additional signals: voice tone, facial expressions, gestures, and posture are among them. Print, in contrast, appears cold, neutral, or potentially hostile.

Humor—especially sarcasm—becomes dangerous. The reader wonders, "Hey, is she kidding or not?"

To assist readers, take extra care with organization, repetition, and simple words. Savvy e-mail writers employ *emoticons*, symbols which mirror the writer's mood. I'm sure you have seen the "smiley faces" made with a colon and the parenthesis sign.

Unhappily, some of us have suffered because e-mail is not retrievable. Once those words fade from your screen, they are gone *irrevocably*. Plus, they emerge in print elsewhere. Once I made a mistake of sending a note to the person I was writing *about*, since she was on my mind. The results weren't funny. Ever since, I have read both the address and the message three or four times before hitting "enter."

Corresponding with strangers may lead to enjoyable and profitable exchanges. Two of my fellow communication professionals have shared helpful information, even though we know each other only through e-mail. One lives in Rhode Island, the other in Canada—yet we communicate with the same camaraderie as though we lunched together often.

Still, caution makes sense. The Internet resembles society—with many intelligent people of high character, along with swindlers and perverts. One consultant withdrew her home address from her site—"too many nuts out there," she decided.

Keep your e-mail messages informal. Purple prose has no place here. Sentences are short, even incomplete. Conversation resembles watercooler talk, not boardroom austerity.

BTW ("by the way" is what this emoticon means), my computer screen uses an exclamation point to let me know I have an unopened e-mail message. I conclude by saying this is highly appropriate. I become as excited by that mark as I ever did by seeing a letter in my mailbox.

YOUR WEB SITE—AN ELECTRONIC BROCHURE

REMEMBER WHEN YOU FIRST HEARD ABOUT WEB sites? Did you think they were reserved for large corporations or wealthy individuals? As you became more familiar with the Internet, you found your first impression was wrong. You discovered dozens of Web sites created by average people who want to display their ideas, services, or products to a wide audience.

After viewing an old movie on television, I did a "Net search" on Jennifer Jones, who starred in the film. I found a thorough, colorful Web site, tracing her biography and movie career. My e-mail to the site's host prompted his reply that he had never met Jennifer Jones or even corresponded with her. Apparently, he invested considerable time, money, and creativity in the site in order to share his admiration with a wide public.

So think of your site as an *electronic brochure*. Just as you work with printers to produce promotional pieces, you'll rely on Internet providers to display your themes, goods, and services.

Your site enjoys advantages the printed brochure can't offer. You can make changes easily at moderate cost. The number of copies you generate is limitless. You don't need postage. There's no delay in delivery—just say, "Here's how you can access my site, even while we're talking on the phone." You or the viewer can print "hard copies" for only the price of the paper.

In promoting my speaking and training business, I rely on my site to the exclusion of standard brochures. In their place, I have a few "one sheets," featuring speech and workshop topics. However, my site contains the same information in condensed form.

Let's say you're planning to establish your own site, for personal and/or business reasons. What do marketing experts tell us about making our site attractive enough to guarantee attention?

First: Include graphics. Keep in mind how *visually dependent* we have become. Two year olds want video games for birthday gifts, not the motionless toys their parents enjoyed. By the time we're adults, we've moved from cartoons to highly volatile movies to flashy commercials. To inform, educate, or persuade us, you have to catch—and hold—our attention with color, movement, and sound.

What happens when you pull up a site and see nothing but writing? Think about the times you've stayed in a hotel during a convention, and tuned to the channel that runs the printed schedule on the screen. Hard to watch, isn't it? Without an appeal to the imagination, the mind wanders. You move to another channel, where *something is happening.*

132

Compared to the attention they generate, graphics cost very little. Something as simple as a blinking line invites the eye to that spot. When you add an item, draw the viewer to it with a flashing, bright word in big letters—NEW!

My site opens with my company's logo revolving, the two letters intertwining endlessly. I've seen a transportation company's site featuring a truck moving across the screen.

Second: Make sure the site's copy is letter perfect. You're presenting a display available to millions of potential readers. A typo or misspelling will reflect careless work. Ask your friends and colleagues to proofread your site's message.

Even with these precautions, mistakes happen. Twice I've had readers call my attention to omitted or inverted letters. I thank them graciously, and call my provider to request instant correction.

Third: When your site is a business site, focus on how you serve people. Sure, you need to say enough about yourself to establish your credentials. List your qualifications and include testimonials from happy clients. Yet the main question prospective clients ask is not "Who are you?" but "What can you do for me?" Tell them simply—and repeatedly.

Fourth: Include your contact information. As you'd do with a printed brochure, provide your mailing address, e-mail (hyperlinked, preferably), phone, and fax. Occasionally, I'll be highly impressed with someone's site—then amazed by the omission of a phone number.

Fifth: Exercise good taste. Until someone meets you, *your site is you.* Avoid comments and quips which could offend a group. Let others applaud you through endorsement letters, but be careful about commending yourself.

Follow these suggestions—then send me the URL that will guide me to your site. Undoubtedly, then I'll receive helpful pointers from you.

SINGING OFF THE SAME PAGE

IN THE SOUTHERN SECTION OF THE UNITED STATES, people will say, "We have to make sure we're all singing off the same page." I suppose this popular saying started in a religious setting. Imagine a choir or congregation singing, with some group members using one music page and the rest singing from another page. Predictably, disharmony and confusion would replace the intended synchronized sounds.

When a business or industry equips a large percentage of employees with computers, managers make this investment to facilitate *coordinated communication*. If every decision maker has access to the same information, then the organization will sing the same tune and use the same words.

Sounds nice, right? Unfortunately, even companies who have gone high tech continually demonstrate disorganization.

My wife and I ordered a filing cabinet from a store located just seven miles from our house. Ironically, this is the store where we bought our computer—a place we'd expect to practice coordinated communication.

Store officials told us they didn't provide delivery. They gave us an 800 number to call (at an unidentified location). What followed was frustrating, inefficient, and obviously disjointed. The first person who answered informed us the delivery could take as long as two weeks. Remember, throughout the two weeks, this cabinet was on display in a store less than fifteen minutes drive from our house.

We didn't hear for ten days, so we called back. To our amazement, no one was aware our order existed, or even that we had called previously. "Not listed in our computer," a representative muttered without emotion. We started all over again, giving model, color, and style, along with the credit card number.

During the third week, a caller promised delivery. "When?" I asked, explaining no one would be at my house during the day unless we knew the exact arrival time.

"Oh, we can't tell you for sure. You see, our delivery truck doesn't have a phone, and we never know exactly where it is."

"But as I said, it's necessary for me to know. Otherwise, no one will be there to open the house."

"All right, we'll make it Wednesday, mid-afternoon."

No one showed up. On Thursday morning I headed to my car to begin an out of town trip. A delivery truck blocked my driveway. The driver asked, "Are you the guy who's expecting a filing cabinet?"

"Sure am," I answered.

"Well, we tried to deliver yesterday. But we went to Dahlonega, thinking you lived there." Dahlonega is twenty-five miles away.

No need to argue or complain. However, I did suggest that a phone in the delivery truck could improve contact with the home office and the customer.

"Yeah, we might get one."

While the two men unpacked the cabinet, two phone calls reflected the communication problems plaguing the store.

First call: "Sir, we're sorry to tell you, but we can't deliver your filing cabinet until tomorrow."

Second call: "Has your filing cabinet arrived yet?"

My head was spinning from those calls when the delivery man said, "Say, I gotta show you where the cabinet was damaged when we stacked it in the truck." He pointed to a dent I might not have seen on my own.

"Want me to take this one back, and have you order another one?" he offered. You can imagine how quickly I declined. Thankfully, he eased my discomfort by arranging a thirty dollar discount.

Obviously, this nationally known store maintained inadequate records. Despite highly developed computer systems, communication between employees seemed either nonexistent or conflicting. Not only were these people on different pages, the customer wondered whether anybody had a song book.

The major lesson here: technology *assists* managers in coordinating communication. To use the equipment to full advantage requires tedious steps—meetings, memos, explanation of policies, careful data storage, easy access to information.

How well does your organization coordinate the internal and external communication made possible by computers? Grade yourself honestly, then move toward eliminating confusion.

THE INTERNET—AN INTERNATIONAL CONSUMERS' FORUM

RALPH NADER BECAME ONE OF THE FIRST internationally known consumer advocates with the 1965 publication of his book *Unsafe at Any Speed*. He charged that automobile manufacturers built cars for style and for their own profit, without concern for safety.

An excellent communicator, Nader appeared on many radio and television programs. He spoke to college audiences and consumer protection groups.

One interesting contrast between the 1960s and now is the way a disgruntled consumer reaches a vast audience. Then you had to write a book, and hope your book would make bestseller lists, as Nader's did. Now, everybody can draw national attention if they have access to the computer and know how to utilize the Internet.

Consider the case of a lady who got upset when a video rental store charged her a ten-dollar late fee. She protested. The store didn't accept her explanation. Repeatedly, she tried to resolve the problem by telephone. Still, bill collectors hounded her.

Annoyed beyond description, she went to the Internet, posting her story on what's called a "bulletin board." Her comment: "Five minutes of my time to complain to thousands of people is a good turnaround."

Her complaint worked, rather quickly. The company's national headquarters sent her an apology—and a gift certificate. The vice president for operations admitted the obvious: "The Internet has become a very powerful consumer tool."

Those who supply goods and services need to remain aware of the massive audience available to aggravated customers. We're not talking about someone who writes a hot letter to the editorial page of the local newspaper. We're going beyond the individual who becomes a guest on your town's talk-radio station. Multiply the impact of those communication channels thousands of times in order to estimate the magnitude of spreading bad news through cyberspace.

From the opposite vantage point, the consumer welcomes opportunities to talk to millions of people within seconds. Maybe I'm not exaggerating in saying our society now has millions of Ralph Naders, instead of the one we had almost four decades ago.

9

MEDIA

OVERHEARD ALMOST ANYWHERE: "HAS THE PAPER come yet?"

"Guess what I heard on my car radio on the way to work!"

"What's on the other channel, dear?"

"Gotta believe it. It was on the front page of the paper."

"Cancel our subscription. They've gotten too liberal for us."

"Good news is that they covered our story. Bad news is that they misquoted us terribly."

"I keep sending stuff to them, but they won't print it."

"Those news folks don't tell us anything good anymore— just crime and accidents and fires."

"I turned down the invitation. Just too scared to be interviewed by that guy."

"What'll we do tonight? Looks like cable won't be back on."

Radio, television, newspapers, and magazines supply an overwhelming percentage of our information, entertainment, culture, sports, and perception of the world around us. At times we vilify them, at other times we deify them.

Dealing with the media successfully isn't so tough if you use the checklist this chapter summarizes. These how-tos will equip you to avoid public catastrophe—and work with media representatives as your *advocates*, not your adversaries.

137

FAMILIAR FACES, VOICES, AND PAGES

HAVE YOU EVER MOVED FROM ONE CITY TO ANOTHER? If so, you're familiar with the numerous adjustments involved, especially when you bring a family—new schools, new workplaces, new neighborhoods, new directions to follow, new places of worship.

Early in my career, I moved often enough to experience these problems repeatedly. Yet I haven't mentioned one of the toughest adjustments—getting accustomed to new media personalities.

Think about it. Ordinarily you start your day, and maybe end it, hearing news, weather and sports, or reading about them. For years, you've read the same editorial writers and listened to the same broadcasters. You consider them longtime guests in your home—in print, and by audio and video transmission.

So when you confront unfamiliar voices, faces, and newspaper columnists, you feel unsettled, out of place. You've heard people say, "I still subscribe to the newspaper in the city I left (or read it on the Internet every day). I don't know many people there now, but I just feel comfortable with the paper I read for years."

As for radio, through the Internet you can tune into stations around the country, if your computer offers this accessory. Imagine listening to the morning program you heard during breakfast for a decade or so.

Really, frequent travelers encounter a similar sense of displacement. The Atlanta native who goes to Des Moines for a week misses the media friends back home.

This is one reason I think CNN television enjoys worldwide popularity. Almost anywhere you go, you can still see the same faces, hear the same voices. Through the magic of satellites, they remain in touch. When my wife and I unpacked in Puerto Villarta, Ixtapa, Cancun, and Aruba, we were delighted to have some of our favorite broadcasters welcome us soon after we reached our rooms.

Personally, I appreciate the continuity our media friends give us. Life throws so many changes our way, we welcome those individuals who remain constant. I hope they understand how much we enjoy their faces, voices, and words as they interpret the world's events to us every day. Consider dropping them handwritten notes to express your gratitude.

FANTASY FULFILLED

DID YOU EVER FANTASIZE ABOUT BECOMING A radio disc jockey? Many people do, and I was among them. "Farmer Jim" Neal in Jackson, Mississippi, served as my early idol. Jim shared homespun humor, sprinkled with comments about community activities and colorful personalities.

When I became a university faculty member, my DJ dream seemed to grow dim. "I'm too busy," I reasoned. "Wouldn't fit my professorial role, either."

Still, I continued to identify with favorite record-spinners, and envy them. Just in case, I earned a broadcaster's license.

Then my chance came. Moving to a small town in Kansas, I noticed there was only one radio station. I'd heard you have to start small in the media, so I approached the station manager.

"I can work nights and weekends," I told Claude.

"Good," he said. "Be here at five on Saturday morning." I gulped, agreed, and showed up as scheduled.

Claude ushered me through the studio, explaining that while I ran the AM "board" as a DJ, I'd monitor the automated FM equipment, changing tapes periodically. I got dizzy, looking at the complex equipment. To be honest, the orientation overwhelmed me. Claude shattered my preconceived notions about casually searching record collections and preparing newscasts. However, I wasn't going to miss my opportunity.

To keep my employer from knowing I was moonlighting, I proposed, "Claude, I won't use my real name. I'll be Ed Watson—that's my middle name and my wife's maiden name."

"Sounds good. We'll go with it."

The station crew grew accustomed to the name before I could. When they'd say, "Morning, Ed" in the hallway, I'd turn to see who was behind me.

Several memories of the Ed Watson days (which lasted two years) remain vivid.

I won't forget the long hours. On Saturdays and Sundays, I started at noon and went until midnight. The AM shut down at dark. Then I recorded commercials. How many times did I blooper one word, then have to start over?

I remember the interesting DJs I worked with. There was Jay (a name duplicated by hundreds of DJs nationwide), whose deaf-mute parents would never hear his broadcasts. There was Bob, who led a popular local band. There was Ken, who tried to use the motto for my show—"With Music As Lovely As a Kansas Sunset." Jay let him know the saying belonged to me alone. After all, I created it.

I remember the fun of giving away prizes, hearing my commercials as I drove home, and answering song requests.

I remember the pay. Minimum wage, so a year's work brought in a thousand dollars. Possibly I would have paid that much for the fun.

A professional move ended my time at KNEX. I recall my final sign-off (not as memorable or as celebrated as David Brinkley's). After expressing appreciation to the station management and to listeners, I chose a record whose title relayed my thoughts—Gloria Gaynor's *I Never Can Say Goodbye*.

McPherson, Kansas, has forgotten my finale. But I still blush when I recall starting Gloria's record on the wrong speed.

UNNECESSARY NUMBERS

ON RADIO AND TELEVISION, AND IN NEWSPAPERS and magazines, you'll hear and read sentences like these:

"Hartex Industries names George Justice, 58, CEO and President, replacing Tom Bolin, 63, who had held the position since 1991."

"Janet Ellis, 38, will become President of New Horizons Travel on September 1."

"The jury acquitted forty-seven-year-old Warren Wilson on the charge of armed robbery."

What's wrong with these news leads? They contain unnecessary numbers. The releases should omit the ages of the people mentioned. Why? Because age represents just another personal characteristic we don't choose and can't change. Using a parallel approach, the reporters could have told us about "blue-eyed George Justice," "long-armed Tom Bolin," "five-foot-four-inch Janet Ellis," and "redheaded Warren Wilson."

Now, I'll admit that print and nonprint media have made commendable strides in recent years, removing other instances of slanted language.

Consider racial references. For many decades, mentioning minorities did not include proper titles. Courageous editors and announcers changed the pattern. I remember when an upset reader phoned his editor and asked, "Why did you refer to the black woman in the article as *Mrs.*?" Without hesitating, the editor answered, "Because she is married." Titles of courtesy were slow in coming, and they're so commonplace now we tend to forget the struggle for media recognition.

Think about gender-related stories. Instead of the outmoded headline "Woman Heads Bank Board," today's newspaper prints "Nelle Jarvis Heads Bank Board."

I applaud publishers and program directors for affirming that race and gender deserve nonjudgmental treatment, on the air and on the page.

Yet journalists fail to show similar regard for age. Long after our nation barred age discrimination, writers and broadcasters continue to nourish this bias. The time has come to exert leadership in this arena—by eliminating age references and thus illustrating that most of the time, age doesn't matter.

Certainly when an athlete becomes the youngest winner of the Masters golf tournament, and a senator qualifies as the oldest astronaut, then I'll accept telling audiences about twenty-one-year-old Tiger Woods and seventy-seven-year-old John Glenn. Those achievements are unique, and therefore newsworthy. In these cases, we're dealing with necessary numbers.

Otherwise, journalists should avoid broadcasting and printing irrelevant—and potentially prejudicial—age identification.

What's the custom with your local media?

Say, should you consider writing one of those letters to the editor that we discuss in the last segment of this chapter?

BE MY GUEST

YOU DON'T HAVE TO BE A CELEBRITY TO APPEAR AS a guest on radio and television shows. Really, there aren't enough celebrities to fill the thousands of slots available daily. Producers and hosts *need* the rest of us.

When Dr. Wayne Dyer toured the country as an unknown writer to promote his first book, *Your Erroneous Zones,* he guested on interview shows from one coast to the other. Anonymous as he was, he still found slots almost anywhere. He concluded, "You'll get air time if you offer something rather elementary . . . such as a new recipe for avocado dip."

First-time appearances strike fear into the hearts of typical guests. It's amazing how the most talkative folks go blank when confronted by a microphone.

Having hosted shows, and having been a guest frequently, I'll share a few pointers.

Prior to the show, send the host your list of "sample questions." The majority of hosts welcome your preparation. They reserve the freedom to deviate from the list, and will. Even so, they are likely to pose several questions you provide.

Use your "natural" voice. Guests tend to increase volume, try to project more forcefully, often as imitations of incredible voices they hear on radio and TV. This is not necessary. The equipment will magnify your ordinary speaking level.

In fact, bombastic, boisterous speaking *dims* your voice quality. The receiving equipment gears down, to keep the speaker within an acceptable decibel range.

Granted, you want to avoid mumbling. Be assured, though, when your interviewer hears you plainly, listeners will too, assuming you're sitting the right distance from the mike (or your lapel mike is placed properly).

Most of the time, you'll have a *sound check.* Those controlling the audio are looking for the volume you'll use during the program. Stay close to what you use for testing, and you're fine.

Remember, we are describing interviews, *not* speeches. Our goal is to answer in sentences, avoiding long paragraph or full-page answers. Stations lose audiences with monologues.

People tune in for *interaction.*

At the other extreme, one-word answers are taboo. The guest who responds with "yes," "no," "probably," "uh-huh" turns the show back to the host too abruptly. The host is looking for, "Yes, and here are my reasons for endorsing the proposal."

In normal conversations, people fear pauses. Our anxiety about pauses magnifies when we go on the air. We picture thousands of people muttering, "Has this guy forgotten the question, or gone blank?" Luckily, we're allowed three or four seconds to ponder the question. Use the interval when you must to find the right words. I say "when you must," because pausing after every question could reduce the desired vitality.

As with other public speaking, talk—and don't read. Reading will sound like reading, unless you have extraordinary skills. Confine your reading to verbatim quotations, facts you haven't memorized, and position statements where the wrong word damages the material's integrity.

In using notes, avoid turning pages loudly. You can bring notes to your TV interview and place them inconspicuously— on your lap or a nearby table. Obviously, use large print to prevent squinting and searching.

Should you gesture? That depends on what you do in daily conversation. Talkers who gesture in bridge table chitchat will feel "at home" by gesturing on the show. Facing the television camera, limit your gestures, making them close to the body to stay within camera range.

Clothing matters little with radio. Television guests have wide latitude, depending upon the show's format, which of course you'd check. Stay away from red (it *bleeds* on the screen), iridescent clothing whose images flutter, mismatched colors, gaudy material. A general rule: this is no style show. You want viewers to remember your content, not the package.

My final suggestion: demonstrate vigor, zest, commitment to your subject. Before you take your turn, tune into TV and talk radio for a few days. You'll gain increased respect for guests who transmit energy. Listeners keep the dials fixed on those programs.

Try my suggestions, and your guest shot will be fascinating, fun, and professionally beneficial.

KEY FACTORS IN CRISIS COMMUNICATION

NOBODY PLANS EMERGENCIES. IF THEY DID, WE wouldn't have any. Who'd want them? Emergencies come as surprises, as intruders.

Private, personal crises—death or serious injury come to mind—are handled privately, with assurance brought by family and friends.

On the other hand, organizational crises attract a crowd. Sometimes the crowd includes radio, television, and newspaper reporters. They don't wait for your invitation, nor do they accept your decline. So knowing how to deal with the media effectively when calamity strikes your organization is a must.

Here's a personal experience to show the value of preparation. When I was vice president of a college, I agreed to serve as acting president during the president's absence. The assignment seemed nonthreatening, for the students had left for spring vacation. What, I reasoned, could go wrong in one weekend anyway?

My phone rang—only twenty minutes after I came home Friday afternoon. Within a minute, I found how mistaken my prediction of tranquility had been. Two students (a male and female, unmarried but living together) who didn't leave town for the holidays (I forgot about that possibility) had become the center of revenge that turned to tragedy. For months, I learned, they had been trafficking in drugs. On this fateful Friday, a few of their customers returned to the apartment, complaining about high prices and demanding a refund. A fight erupted, then shooting. The young man died, the girl survived and now lay in a local hospital bed.

The next forty-eight hours thrust me into public pandemonium. As spokesperson for the college, I dealt with print and nonprint media. Reporters demanded details, explanations. "To what extent is the college to blame?" they asked.

Twenty years later, I shudder when, in memory, I relive the trauma of that weekend. I'm sure my dramatic introduction to media relations lies behind the one-day workshop I teach on crisis communication. Consider these key pointers my workshops present and illustrate:

144

First: Organizations must establish media relationships well before they're needed most. To wait until trouble arrives compares to brushing your teeth only on the morning of your dental appointment—problems will surface.

Fortunately, my role at the college had enabled me to become friendly with broadcasters and writers for more than a year before catastrophe hit the school. My face and voice were familiar, so I wasn't a stranger asking for fair play.

Cultivate the media through tours, briefings, regular press releases, inclusion in milestone events.

Second: Organizations must write and distribute a plan for crisis communication. Sadly, the college did not have one. My direction came from instinct and quick advice from a few associates. I'm convinced we made a few serious mistakes which a plan of action could have prevented.

Third: Without delay, provide information the media can make public. Never delay, because delay fosters distrust.

Fourth: Let employees and staff know who speaks for the organization and who doesn't. More than one messenger creates confusion, then suspicion. Automatically, the press and the public expect the CEO to step forward to admit the problem, explain who's responsible, and outline solutions. CEO's master the art of delegation—*but the CEO cannot assign this function to anyone else.*

Fifth: Tell the truth, without dilution or withholding. Especially during critical situations, "little white lies" mushroom into loss of credibility, even public hostility. Avoid "no comment." Without declining blatantly, buy extra time with "we're gathering information on the matter now."

Sixth: Take control of interviews and press conferences. You have a right to say *where, when, who'll be included, and to set the time limits.* Assert your leadership instantly, and don't relinquish it.

Seventh: Videotape conversations with the media. The tapes will become valuable later when someone charges, "I remember what you said." Particularly when lawsuits might erupt, you have an advantage in being able to resurrect your comments.

Eighth: Never enter combat against reporters. Keep this wise slogan in mind: "Never argue with the person who buys ink by the barrel."

Ninth: Debrief your colleagues after the event. Discuss how effectively you implemented your crisis communication plan, remaining open to suggestions for improvement for the next misfortune.

Tenth: Utilize your good media relations *after the crisis subsides*. Issue news releases (a term preferable to "press releases") to talk about successful resolution of the urgent situation. Invite readers and listeners to the facility, to see how you have restored order. Thank media figures for their thorough, accurate coverage.

Clearly, these ten suggestions provide only the framework of what I say in a full training day with an organization's leaders. However, these recommendations will help organizations move toward an effective crisis communication plan—which I hope you never need as badly as I once did.

LETTERS TO THE EDITOR—VOICES OF THE PEOPLE

WHEN YOU READ A NEWSPAPER, WHICH SECTION do you read first? Sports, business, society, world news, local news?

Frequently, the editorial pages catch my attention. Yes, I read the editorials. But before that, I read the letters to the editor.

Why? Because these letters come from the heartland. Instead of representing the editorial staff's position, letters to the editor originate among people largely untrained in journalism. Yet, while the authors might not win a Pulitzer Prize for language skills, the letters carry strong appeal because (with rare exceptions) the writers speak for themselves only, not an organization.

So we're likely to find controversy in this section, with all sorts of potential targets for criticism. Targets include the newspaper itself, local and national government, the school system, corporate officials, developers, religious groups—the list extends endlessly.

Probably you've noticed that your newspaper publishes a few letter writers regularly. Eventually, we know what message to expect when we see the author's name. He or she has one cause to champion, over and over again. We almost think we know these writers.

Have you ever written a letter to the editor? Maybe we say, "I disagree with that action, and I'm going to write a protest letter." Or, "I'm going to voice my support for this good cause." But do we?

When you reach for your stationery, here's what you can expect with most editorial pages:

Letters have word limits. Call to find the allowable number, realizing editors won't make exceptions.

Editors reserve the right to edit for grammatical accuracy and spelling. Some editors change phrases, combine sentences, and omit useless passages. In this regard, resist pride of authorship. Welcome those who help you present a correct image.

Anonymous letters go into the wastebasket. Editors want writers who endorse their thoughts proudly. Either sign or don't send.

Whatever title you suggest, expect the editor to publish another one. Having written for newspapers for many years, I recall only a few times when my articles or letters carried the original title. Not surprisingly, most times I thought mine was more descriptive, even catchier. You will, too, I suppose. Let's remember who owns the paper.

There's no requirement for editors to publish every letter. When hundreds of readers write about a hot issue, and many of the arguments are similar, editors select those which represent the range of opinions. When your letters don't make the printed page, keep this in mind.

To end with a positive tone: Editors want and need articulate, thoughtful letters, particularly those expressing diverse viewpoints. I assure you they welcome such submissions.

Using these guidelines, I encourage you to join the thousands of citizens who enliven newspapers with their candid opinions. Write—and you'll enjoy one of the marvelous privileges of a free press.

YOUR PERSONAL INVITATION
TO CONTACT THE AUTHOR

DR. LAMPTON ENCOURAGES READERS TO SEND their comments and questions to:

> Dr. William Lampton
> P. O. Box 908267
> Gainesville, GA 30501-0920

To review descriptions of his speeches and seminars, check his Web site at http://www.commlampton.com

Bill welcomes opportunities to speak at conferences, conventions, commencements, planning retreats, and other organizational functions. Additionally, he is available for directing workshops and providing consulting services.

You may call him at 800-393-0114, or send e-mail to drbill@commlampton.com